What Others ~~Are Saying~~
Unexpected Journeys:

"With exceptional subtlety and clarity, Paul Perkins unfurls a lifetime of personal hurdles that are—one by one, chapter by chapter—overcome with crystalline Christian conviction and personal humility. This memoir is endlessly inventive as Perkins takes the reader on an epic global journey that is, at once, a journey into the very heart of God. With crisp brio, Perkins allows the reader to be swept up again and again in the moment, and always animated by his sensitivity and transparency. As a writer, he has a wondrous touch."

—Tim Goeglein
Senior adviser, Focus on the Family

"Brave and raw, Paul tells his unfolding adventure with honest self-reflection. His stellar writing style kept me turning the pages. And his discoveries about God, love, and life inspired. A great read."

—Lara Williams
Speaker and author
LaraWilliams.org

"Paul's voice is honest, broken, and still hopeful. His story, emotional and raw…, is a universal one that reveals the presence of a faithful and loving God through our suffering. This is a beautiful, redemptive work."

—Kevin Palau
President, Luis Palau Association
Author, *Unlikely*

"This book is the story of a...[guy] who went halfway around the world, where he discovered God's unmerited favor. Paul shares the tragic experiences that cauterized his heart—and the unexpected ways God broke through."

—*David Murrow*
Author, *Why Men Hate Going to Church*

"Paul Perkins magically cloaks the reader in a refreshingly honest story of adventure, redemption, and the creative spirit inside all of us. *Unexpected Journeys* is a candid account of big ideas in a small world."

—*Marty Makary, MD*
New York Times best-selling author, *Unaccountable*

"*Unexpected Journeys* is more than a tale of a twentysomething's travel through Asia—it brings to life what we know to be true: that even in the deepest of valleys, God is working for our good. Paul Perkins's writing is authentic, honest and captivating. I enthusiastically recommend this book!"

—*Marc Vaillancourt*
Blogger and host of *The Conversation Hub* podcast

"There are some books that, when you're finished reading them, you put them down and go on living life. But then there are other books with such storytelling depth that when you finish reading them, you can't help but pause and reconsider the story you're living. *Unexpected Journeys* is this sort of book. I'm thankful for the story God gave Paul, and that Paul had the courage to pen it down."

—*Neal Samudre*
Creator of EssentialHustle.com

"Paul Perkins's spiritual memoir offers an inspiring story of self-discovery and spiritual healing, in which Christian faith prevails against despair. Some in his generation ponderously critique the faith they inherited. In contrast, Paul courageously recounts how he finally found deliverance through divine grace."

—*Mark Tooley*
President, Institute on Religion and Democracy

"My White House colleague Paul Perkins has written a book filled with honesty, feeling, and hard-gained wisdom. *Unexpected Journeys* is the moving testimony of a good man. It will be a blessing to everyone who reads it."

—*John P. McConnell*
Former Deputy Assistant and
Senior speechwriter to President George W. Bush

"From the halls of the White House to the back streets of Thailand, Paul Perkins takes the reader on a journey around the world. Despite the number of miles traveled and the exotic locales visited, the greater exploration takes place within. Readers will enjoy the travel adventures, but they will really be moved by the personal transformation."

—*John M. Persinger*
Author, *The Saint Joseph Plot*

"Paul lays it all out, giving a totally vulnerable and heartfelt account of his trip through Southeast Asia. I know God is everywhere but I think he really reveals himself when you go out on a limb like Paul did."

—*Connor Martin*
Front man, Con Bro Chill

"In this deeply personal story, Paul Perkins takes us on a physical adventure to ask the deep questions of the soul, and in doing so wrestles with issues of friendship, failure, pain, and loneliness. Ultimately, his story unveils the need for an authentic relationship with God. *Unexpected Journeys* is a must-read for anyone searching for personal truth."

—*Gary Witherall*
Author, *Total Abandon*
Serving with Operation Mobilization

"An honest look at how to navigate the unexpected junk life throws you, and how faith can impact that junk in a positive way. I thoroughly enjoyed reading every page of Paul's adventure."

—*Justin Scott*
Young Life Area Director, Bend, Oregon

"I love *Unexpected Journeys*. It's interesting, vulnerable, extremely relatable, and intensely personal. It penetrates to the heart of many of my fears and struggles both now and in the past. I'm grateful to Paul for sharing his life with us."

—*Francis Floth*
Cru Missional Team Leader
University of California, Davis

UNEXPECTED JOURNEYS

PAUL PERKINS

WHITAKER
HOUSE

All Scripture quotations are taken from the *Holy Bible, New International Version*®, NIV®, © 1973, 1978, 1984, 2011 by Biblica, Inc.® Used by permission. All rights reserved worldwide.

UNEXPECTED JOURNEYS:
My Search for Adventure, Love, and Redemption on the Other Side of the World

paulperkins.com

ISBN: 978-1-62911-699-0
eBook ISBN: 978-1-62911-700-3
Printed in the United States of America
© 2016 by Paul Perkins

Whitaker House
1030 Hunt Valley Circle
New Kensington, PA 15068
www.whitakerhouse.com

Published in association with literary agent David Van Diest Literary Agency.
www.christianliteraryagency.com

Author photograph by Cedric Terrell.

Library of Congress Cataloging-in-Publication Data

Names: Perkins, Paul, 1981- author.
Title: Unexpected journeys : my search for adventure, love, and redemption on the other side of the world / by Paul Perkins.
Description: New Kensington, PA : Whitaker House, 2016.
Identifiers: LCCN 2016004749 (print) | LCCN 2016008367 (ebook) | ISBN 9781629116990 (trade pbk. : alk. paper) | ISBN 9781629117003 (eBook)
Subjects: LCSH: Perkins, Paul, 1981—Travel—Southeast Asia. | Perkins, Paul, 1981—Travel—India. | Southeast Asia—Description and travel. | Indonesia—Description and travel. | Thailand—Description and travel. | India—Description and travel. | Voyages around the world. | Travel—Psychological aspects. | Redemption.
Classification: LCC DS522.6 .P38 2016 (print) | LCC DS522.6 (ebook) | DDC 910.4/1—dc23
LC record available at http://lccn.loc.gov/2016004749

1 2 3 4 5 6 7 8 9 10 11 **W** 23 22 21 20 19 18 17 16

To Hilary

CONTENTS

AUTHOR'S NOTE

I'm a private person. Perhaps that seems strange coming from the author of a memoir. But still, it's true. I've never been the sort of guy who wears his emotions on his sleeve. I even have a hard time opening up to friends, sharing my successes and failures, let alone my wounds and flaws.

I know a lot of guys feel the same way. But for me it's not so much a cultural thing. I don't think lowering my guard makes me less of a man or anything. In fact, the men I admire most are vulnerable with their past and expressive of their emotions. That's because vulnerability isn't weakness. It's strength.

Like I said, though, it doesn't come naturally for me.

I mention this because I want you to know this book wasn't easy to write. I'm not sure any book is ever easy, but this one, my first to get published, required more than I thought I could give. Every chapter pushed me beyond my comfort zone. Some stories brought me to tears.

Why, then, am I sharing it with the world? Why am I putting myself out there when I would prefer to lay low? Why am I stepping into the spotlight?

It's simple, really. I believe in the power of redemption. That where we are weakest, where we are broken, where we have been wounded, is actually where we have the greatest power. It's a paradigm shift, an upside-down perspective, yet I feel its truth in my bones. It's taken me a long time to embrace this lesson. I'm still embracing it, actually.

So that's why I wrote this book. Not because I want my stories floating out there, resting between strangers' hands and gathering dust on bookshelves. But because I believe that by sharing my stories—these strung-together words representing my deepest, most profound life experiences—I can nudge even one person closer to wholeness and joy.

Plus, I'm confident you'll have fun reading it. I certainly enjoyed living it.

PART ONE
INDONESIA

1

TIME OF MY LIFE

Elephants captivate me.

I don't say that because a GOP elephant sticker adorned my car's steering wheel while in college and, a year after graduating, I landed my dream job at the White House working for President George W. Bush.

Rather, I say it because ever since watching *Dumbo* as a kid, I've seen elephants sort of like humans stuck in dinosaur-like bodies. If I had one, I imagined it'd be my best friend and strongest defender—protecting me from my scariest enemies.

But I'd pretty much given up on meeting one up close; according to travel guides, most elephant camps are inhumane. Then, halfway through my journey around the world, I happened upon an elephant sanctuary in northern Thailand. And to my surprise, it checked out. The animals were well-cared for and happy.

At first I stood back and just watched as they snatched bananas from peoples' hands and crushed branches with their trunks. Then I grabbed a banana and held it in front of the largest elephant, Hallel. He didn't take it, so I stepped directly under his gaping mouth and tossed it inside. He swallowed with a *galumph*.

Before I had a chance to step back, Hallel wrapped his trunk around my chest and squeezed tight. Fearful he might suffocate me, I looked to his trainer who smiled.

"It's okay. He hug you."

When Hallel's grip loosened, the trainer asked, "You want to ride?"

I thought he was joking, but then the giant knelt to the ground. I eagerly climbed onto his back. His skin felt rough and hard like a leather shield. Hair as thick as wire sparsely covered his body and droopy ears flapped back and forth, fanning his face and body, and keeping insects away.

As Hallel walked down a wide dirt pathway, slowly shifting his weight side to side, I grasped onto his wrinkles, afraid of falling ten feet and ruining the rest of my trip with a broken leg. When the elephant spotted a vegetation-covered bush, he bolted toward it. Just as quickly he lurched to a stop, then pulverized the thing with his trunk and stuffed a boatload of leaves into his mouth.

Soon Hallel spotted another bush and rushed toward it. "Slow down," I yelled, holding on for dear life. But he didn't seem to hear me. So I surrendered to his will—I trusted him with my life, or at least my limbs, and tried to enjoy the ride.

Once he finished snacking, Hallel ambled over to a nearby river and waded in until his body was half submerged. I wondered if cartoons I'd seen as a kid were true—surely elephants don't squirt water out of their trunks, do they? No sooner had the thought crossed my mind than his trunk swung behind his head. Before I could move, two-and-a-half gallons of water sprayed into my face—completely soaking me.

Hallel then dropped his head, dunking me into the water and lifting me out again. It seemed like the perfect opportunity to do something I'd dreamed about doing. I scurried up Hallel's neck and carefully stepped onto his head. Balancing on the lumpy but stable platform, I stood tall and, for a few seconds, felt at one with the mighty beast. Then Hallel shook his head, catapulting me through the air and into the water.

When I popped above the surface, I laughed until my stomach hurt.

Which was nice—playing with old Hallel in the river. Because I hadn't planned it. And the longer I traveled, the more I realized my plans usually interfered with what God was doing. And he was up to something big.

What I really needed to do was hold on tight and enjoy the ride. That proved more difficult than I could've imagined.

MY JOURNEY AROUND THE WORLD BEGAN WHERE I GREW UP—IN Portland, Oregon. On a rainy spring afternoon, my parents dropped me off at the airport and, after hugging them goodbye, I trotted through the terminal carrying my brand-new grey 70-liter backpack, confident I'd just embarked on the adventure of a lifetime.

For five years I had lived in Washington, DC. And while I had a great time there, the frantic pace left me burnt out—I worked full-time by day and by night attended law school at The George Washington University. It was exciting but exhausting.

As soon as I turned in my last exam, I didn't waste any time leaving behind that hectic life. I stuffed my belongings in the backseat of my black Hyundai Elantra and began the cross-country drive back home to Oregon.

My plan was to take out another student loan and rent a sweet studio apartment in downtown Portland. I dreamed of filling it with fancy furniture and hosting parties with interesting friends while I studied for the bar exam on the side. I couldn't wait to start over and create a new life.

The plan was definitely *not* to crash at my parents' house.

I even told my friends before leaving DC that living with my parents was my worst option. Not because there's bad blood or anything. They're wonderful people. It's just that when I'm with my family, whether it's my parents or either of my older brothers, it's like I jump back into the eighth grade picture of me sitting on my parents' dresser—and believe me, that's the last place I want to go.

But while cruising through New Mexico at 70 mph, my phone buzzed in the cup-holder. It was a text from the one person in Oregon I least wanted to hear from—Adam. "Is everything ok?" he asked. I stopped at a gas station to respond.

By the time I pulled back on the freeway, I had decided to stay in Portland no longer than necessary. No studio apartment, no parties. I'd study hard, hopefully pass the bar, then move on—that's it. Because in all my dreaming, I'd overlooked an inconvenient problem: Portland wasn't a new city for me. No matter how hard I tried to make myself believe I could start fresh there, I couldn't. The city had too much history, and for the life of me, I couldn't shed that fact. And that history, my past there, felt too heavy to shoulder.

I needed to get away—far away.

So, I unloaded everything in my parents' garage and took over their guestroom for a couple months. From six in the morning until nine at night, I read and memorized and listened to lectures and took practice tests—and planned the most epic trip I could imagine.

FROM PORTLAND I FLEW TO SAN FRANCISCO. WHILE WAITING FOR MY connecting flight to Hong Kong—and from there, Bali, Indonesia—I called my girlfriend, Alissa. We'd been dating on-and-off for ten months, but recently our relationship had turned serious.

"I'll miss you," Alissa said, her voice a whisper. Never one to be overly emotional, she still didn't seem happy with my decision to travel. She expected, as did many of my friends, that I would return to DC after taking the bar exam.

"I'll miss you too," I said. "But at least we'll see each other in India."

We had dreamed up the idea of reuniting in India during my final week overseas which coincided with a trip she had planned to Kenya. We had no doubt it would be a romantic rendezvous for the history books, the sort of story we would tell our kids and grandkids after growing old and grey.

"That's right. And it's only eleven weeks away," she said, her voice straining to sound optimistic.

"We can make it. We'll write emails. Lots and lots of emails."

She sighed. "Yeah. But I like seeing you in person better."

"Me too." I paused and glanced at the growing line at the gate. "Maybe we can Skype."

"I hope so."

The phone went quiet for a few seconds. I got up. "I better go. I think my plane's about to board."

"Bye, Paul. Let me know when you get there."

"I will. Talk to you soon." I slipped my phone into my pocket, grabbed my backpack, and stepped to the back of the line.

THE MOMENT I WALKED OFF THE PLANE, I DIDN'T NEED ANYONE TO tell me I wasn't in Oregon. The heat felt like a straitjacket squeezing every ounce of sweat from my body. Beads of perspiration emerged on my forehead and above my lip. Everyone wore shorts, t-shirts, and flip-flops. And no one looked like me—pasty white with a charcoal fedora over shaggy dark hair.

At the curbside of the airport, I spotted my friend, Eko. Indonesian by birth, Eko spent twelve years in the United States. We met soon after I moved to DC at the Anglican church we both attended. Although he was at least fifteen years older than almost everyone else, no one treated him differently—he was too nice and unassuming not to like, the type of person you immediately felt comfortable around. At the same time, you couldn't help feeling bad for the guy. For whatever reason he couldn't hold a steady job, and he rarely had his own place, but instead slept on friends' couches.

Eventually, he moved into a house I shared with some friends. It was fun having another roommate around, especially someone known to cook a mean Top Ramen with egg and teriyaki. Some mornings he woke up early just to walk with me to Union Station, keeping me company on my commute.

After a while, Eko started growing distant—at first he stopped staying at our house, then he stopped coming by altogether. It was the same pattern he always followed, but I felt rotten about it, like it had somehow been my fault.

Sometime later he returned to Indonesia and we lost touch. When I began thinking about traveling, he immediately came to mind. I had always wanted to see Indonesia, and I figured it'd be nice to reconnect. After all, I still considered him a friend.

Eko gave me with a hug. "I've missed you, buddy," he said, patting my back and speaking in a thick Javanese accent. He looked older than when I last saw him; wrinkles extended from the corners of his eyes, and his hair, jet black before, now blended grey with black.

"It's great to see you," I said. Not wanting to come across as an overeager tourist, I tried to conceal my excitement and play it cool, but I couldn't. A smile consumed my face.

"Follow me." Eko grabbed my arm, led me across a packed parking lot, and stopped in front of an old motorbike. Scrapes scarred its black plastic body and a faded license plate hung behind the seat.

"It's...nice."

Eko stared at the bike adoringly. "Uh-huh."

"So this is what we're driving around Bali," I said, more as a question than a statement. Although Eko and I were small guys, I couldn't imagine it hauling us around the island with my ginormous backpack strapped to my body. I foresaw myself tipping off the back as we chugged up a hill.

"We will have the greatest time, Paul. I am so happy." Eko hopped on the bike and started the engine, revving it a few times. He looked at me and popped a smile.

I took a deep breath, tightened my backpack straps, and saddled the bike. Gripping the metal seat rail behind me, I held on tight as Eko raced out of the parking lot and toward Kuta Beach, one of the most popular spots in Bali.

We stopped at a food stand on the edge of the beach and, with a view of the Indian Ocean, ate grilled fish and caught up. Since leaving DC, Eko had moved around Indonesia, but he recently settled in a remote village in East Java.

"You'll love it there," he said, his eyes gazing at the ocean. "It's quiet and serene and still—about as unlike DC as you can find."

"Perfect," I said quietly.

As the sun neared the horizon, a sea of people flooded the beach to watch a rainbow of colors transform the sky into a painter's canvas. The sunset felt like a sacred ceremony. A hushed silence descended upon the crowd as waves softly crashed nearby.

Later, while checking email at our hotel, I received a message from a high school friend, Jeremy. Calling him a friend is probably overstating it. One year we played soccer together, but we never actually hung out. He and his surfer buddies were a bit too cool for me. I emailed him several days earlier after hearing he and his wife were in Bali volunteering at an orphanage. He suggested meeting for breakfast the next day, and I said sure.

In the morning, Eko and I woke up early and headed across town to a restaurant called The Balcony. When we arrived, Jeremy was already seated at a table overlooking the raucous street below. He must have heard us walking toward him, because he turned and waved.

"Hey man," Jeremy said, standing up and shaking my hand.

"Good to see you," I said. "This is my friend, Eko. We met in DC, then for some crazy reason he decided to move back here."

Eko and Jeremy laughed as they shook hands. "Haven't regretted it for a minute," Eko said with a smile.

I grinned. "It's not so bad."

Eko and I sat across from Jeremy, and while they got to know each other, I perused the menu. When the waiter came by, Eko and Jeremy ordered, then I asked for nasi goreng and a banana shake.

"So what are you doing out here, Perkins?" Jeremy asked after a while. "I heard you made quite a name for yourself in DC, working at the White House. Why'd you leave?"

"Dude," Eko interrupted, "one time Paul snuck me into the White House and walked me through all the fancy rooms. I was freaking out—I'd overstayed my visa by about ten years."

I laughed awkwardly. "I didn't sneak you in. It was just one of those tour things for staff, and I figured Secret Service was more concerned about catching terrorists than good people like you." I looked at Jeremy and he was chuckling.

"So did you and G' Dub ever kick it in the Oval?" he asked.

"Not quite," I said with a laugh. "But I did occasionally see him around."

"That's cool. You meet anyone else?"

"You mean, like, politicians? Yeah, of course."

"No. I mean cool people."

I laughed. "Well, I met tons of professional athletes and Olympians. Arnold Schwarzenegger. One time I sort of met Brad Pitt. The best, though, was Bono."

Jeremy looked impressed. "That's awesome."

"Yeah, working there was definitely the honor of a lifetime. But someone else got elected so my job disappeared. Then once I finished law school and took the bar exam, I decided to see the world before I jumped back into the rat race."

"I hear ya, man," Jeremy said, shaking his head. "Lucy and I have been out here for half a year, and it's spectacular. The food, the surfing, the people. We love it."

"Yeah? You're helping kids, right?"

Jeremy nodded and said, "They're amazing. Every day they inspire me."

"Wow, that's great. You know, that's something I've always wanted to do."

"You should. It'll change you."

I nodded. "Maybe you're right."

"So," Jeremy said, stretching his arms above his head, "are you dating anyone?"

The thought of Alissa made me smile. "Yup. This great girl in DC."

"Doing the long distance thing?"

I sighed. "Trying."

"That's what Lucy and I did for a while."

"Really? Any words of wisdom?"

Jeremy appeared to consider the question. Then he looked at me seriously. "Do you like her?"

"Yeah." A moment later, "Of course."

"No. I mean, do you *really* like her—as in, she might be The One?"

I thought for a few seconds. "Maybe. I hope."

Jeremy smiled. "Then go all out, man. If you think you two might one day get married, don't hold back. You won't regret it, and she'll appreciate it."

I nodded my head. "That's good. Really good. Thanks." I wasn't flattering him, either. His words moved me, and right then, I determined to follow his advice. Alissa was worth it.

"So what are your plans here?" Jeremy asked.

"We're exploring Bali for a week, then it's on to East Java—where Eko lives. I've gotta get back here in four weeks to catch my flight to Thailand, but otherwise, we'll probably take our time traveling the country."

"Sounds perfect, man. You'll have the time of your life. Indonesia is amazing."

And Jeremy was right—I had the time of my life. Over the next week, Eko and I circled Bali on a motorbike. We slept on beaches, snorkeled with fish, chased dolphins, explored a remote island, and watched a magnificent sunrise and sunset every day. Then we ferried across the Bali Sea and traveled around East Java, mostly by train. From cities and beaches to volcanoes and deserts, we saw it all.

We kept a brisk pace and never planned ahead more than a day, which was exactly as I wanted it. After years of studying and working and anxiety, I needed to hang up the suits and let my hair grow out. I needed to move beyond the rigid role I'd played and enjoy life. I needed to stop avoiding risks and embrace adventure.

But I couldn't shake the feeling I also needed to get away from Eko and head out on my own.

2

MOONWALKING ACROSS JAVA

You might think as a pastor's son I'd be a natural on stage. But I didn't feel like it waiting to address a church full of teenagers. My anxiety grew as Eko spoke, the Javanese flowing from his mouth in a blur. Trying to control my emotions, I took a deep breath and exhaled slowly.

An hour earlier, Eko and I had pulled into the small, bustling city of Kediri to eat dinner with one of Eko's childhood friends, Leo. Soon after we sat down, Leo popped the question: would we speak at his church? It was holding a youth service and he wanted the kids to hear about our adventure. I reluctantly agreed only after Eko got on my case. So while Eko and Leo ate, I jotted down some notes. I figured with a bit of preparation, I could do a respectable job.

Walking into the church, though, I immediately regretted my decision. I came from a tame religious background, without much display of emotion or charisma—there definitely wasn't any banner-waving or interpretive dancing at my dad's church. But watching this service, I felt like I'd stepped into a Benny Hinn crusade. As the band played an energetic worship set, the kids danced wildly, raising their hands and shouting at the top of their lungs.

Near the front of the auditorium, a crowd surrounded a girl, praying in tongues against her animal-like screeches. When the girl saw Leo, she lunged toward him. Eko threw himself in front of his friend, and someone grabbed the girl's thrashing arms.

It gave me a real scare, and I considered making a run for it. But then the music died.

"It's your turn," Leo said, looking at Eko and me.

Eko stepped on stage, and I nervously followed after him. Murmurs trickled through the crowd and a few girls giggled. Standing beside Eko, I mentally ran through my main points while he delivered his remarks. After about ten minutes, he stopped talking and silence filled the auditorium. All eyes locked on me. Looking for guidance, I spotted Leo in the front row. A smile stretched across his face and he gave me a thumbs-up.

"Are you done?" I whispered to Eko.

He nodded. "Yes."

I took a deep breath, glanced down at my notes, then launched into my speech, which was essentially my testimony—a word Christians use to describe the story about how they met God. I wasn't sure how it would translate to Indonesian teenagers, but it was the only speech I could give on the spot.

MY INTRODUCTION TO CHRISTIANITY BEGAN WITH MY ENTRY INTO the world. My parents placed their warm hands on my soft head and prayed God's blessing over me. From that moment forward, faith saturated my life. Every Sunday morning, I woke to the smell of brewing coffee and my dad's booming voice practicing his sermon; then after eating breakfast, my family piled into our navy Oldsmobile and headed to church.

Faith comforted me as a child, and I carried it deep in my soul.

As I grew older, I got involved at church, running slides during worship and inviting friends to youth group. Some of those friends began peppering me with questions about God. To answer their questions, I opened the Bible on my own for the first time. With the harder questions I went to my dad. While he always gave good answers, he did something even better—he pointed me to a stack of apologetics books.

I quickly got my mind around enough information to know my faith wasn't make-believe but based in history. I wasn't satisfied with simple answers, though. I wanted to know more. So I continued studying.

By the time I turned sixteen, I had accumulated tons of data. I knew the New Testament well and could hold my own debating just about any topic a high schooler might raise—whether the historicity of Jesus' resurrection, the inerrancy of the Bible, the scientific support for intelligent design, the differences between Christianity and other religions, or the archeological evidence of biblical events.

Despite all my learning, though, something didn't feel right. That is, I didn't *feel* much of anything. Although I didn't know it at the time, my faith was all brain and no heart. Like learning algebraic formulas, I treated God as just an intellectual belief.

That's not to say my faith wasn't real. In light of my life experiences up to that point, it made sense emotions weren't a part of my faith. But that also meant I had a lopsided faith. God created us as emotional beings, and our relationship with him shouldn't be based on sheer intellectual assent. A vibrant faith requires intellect *and* emotion.

Perhaps more profoundly, my faith as a teenager was wrapped up in my need for stability—my desire to affirm the truth of my childhood and the core of my identity. Adolescence is hard enough, and I certainly wasn't an exception. Like most people, I suffered traumas that left me wounded and scarred. I'm not sure if, in the midst of that turbulent season, I could have also handled a crisis of faith.

So I believed in God because it made sense to believe in God, and because deep down, I needed to continue believing.

It wasn't until years later that my faith began the long, slow descent from my head to my heart. In a sense, I had to journey through the process of decoupling my faith from my personal history. I had to stop seeing Christ through the eyes of a child, a sort of divine Santa Claus, and meet him as an adult. A real man who wanted a real relationship with me.

Over time, I began seeing Christianity differently; less a list of rigid theological doctrines and systematic proofs, and more a dramatic and mysterious love story, a creative explosion inviting everyone to salvation, an overwhelming invitation into the kingdom of heaven—not at some future point in a far-off destination, but right here and right now.

I came to realize that while I had dedicated years to learning about God, I had never really met him. I had studied God's

Word, but I hadn't experienced him. I understood God's nature, but I didn't know him.

As I began drawing near to God, feeling his presence and sensing his Spirit, I noticed it wasn't a result of reading more or memorizing more or studying more. I drew near to God by closing the pages of my Bible and stepping outside, living life in all its glorious messiness.

That's not to minimize the importance of Scripture. It absolutely has its place in the Christian life. God's words are "*sweeter than honey*" (Psalm 19:10). But Scripture isn't everything. In fact, there are countless ways to experience God outside the Bible. In Psalm 19, for instance, the author writes:

> *The heavens declare the glory of God;*
> *The skies proclaim the work of his hands.*
> *Day after day they pour forth speech;*
> *Night after night they reveal knowledge.*
> *They have no speech, they use no words;*
> *No sound is heard from them.*
> *Yet their voice goes out into all the earth,*
> *Their words to the ends of the world.*

While I still identified with the faith of my childhood, in many ways my faith was different. Bigger and more expansive. Deeper and wider. Softer and more flexible. Less defined and more unknown. Spirit-filled and creative. Challenging yet infinitely lighter.

If you think about it, this is a natural progression. Faith is an intrinsically personal experience, and the Christian faith in particular is based on a relationship with the divine. And just like you can't fall in love with a person simply by reading her journal or studying his movements, you can't learn your way into loving God.

You must live with God to love God.

When I finished speaking, I glanced at Eko. He looked confused. "Did you interpret all of that?" I whispered.

Eko looked at me and swallowed hard. "I...tried."

I looked at the crowd. A roomful of blank faces stared back at me. Perhaps I spoke too quickly for Eko to keep up. Or maybe what I said just didn't make sense. Either way, I talked for fifteen minutes and no one, it seemed, had understood a word out of my mouth.

From Kediri, we traveled to Eko's sleepy village deep in the heart of East Java. Surrounded by lush rice fields and soaring mountains, it was as much like paradise as everywhere else we traveled, with one exception—there was nothing to do.

We ended up spending a few days meandering around Eko's house, reading and relaxing and watching roosters strut by on the side of the road. From outside, the one-story structure looked luxurious—it had intact windows, a wood front door, and solid walls.

The inside was a different story. Drywall powder coated everything and none of the rooms had a ceiling, except the bedroom I slept in, which had a plastic tarp hanging between the walls. While all the rooms had doorways, none had doors. The kitchen didn't have appliances either, other than a sink and portable gas stove. The bathroom came equipped with a faucet head sticking out of the wall near the concrete floor, a red bucket for cold baths, and of course a "squatter" toilet—American-style sit-down toilets were unheard of in the village. The only furniture in the house was a large wood dining room table with four ornate chairs. There was, however, a television to watch bootlegged versions of *The Office*.

Time passed slowly. The only excitement came every afternoon when a group of kids and teenagers stopped by the house and gathered in the living room. For the next hour, Eko took them through an English lesson. One time he asked me to introduce myself, and then challenged them to translate what I'd said. I loved seeing their rapt attention and determination. Most of them went home after the lesson, but some stayed and ate dinner with us.

On our last night there, Eko and I drove to an internet café thirty minutes away. As Alissa and I tried to Skype without the benefit of sound—at least we could see each other's face while typing messages back and forth—a boy tapped my shoulder. I turned around and, before I could say a word, he invited Eko and me to visit his madrasa, a traditional Islamic school. I asked Alissa to wait a minute, and Eko and I talked it over. We thought it sounded like a unique experience and said we'd do it.

The next morning, we drove into the walled compound of the madrasa and stopped in the middle of an empty courtyard. I glanced back and saw a giant crescent moon perched high above an iron gate. I immediately felt nervous and wondered if I'd fallen into some sort of trap for western tourists.

But a moment later, my fears eased when the headmaster greeted me with a friendly handshake. He whisked us into his office and directed us to sit on an orange vinyl couch across from him. Then he drew the blinds, instantly darkening the room, and dropped a basket of fruit in front of us.

For half a minute he watched us, then he asked Eko a question. As Eko responded in a hushed whisper, I snacked on slices of star fruit and looked at framed photos of men in military uniforms decorating the walls.

After a while, they began speaking more casually. Then Eko and the headmaster stood and walked toward the door to the courtyard. I tossed a piece of star fruit back into the basket and stood next to Eko.

"This is amazing," he said, turning toward me with the biggest smile.

"What?" I asked.

Just then, the headmaster grasped my arm and walked us outside, up a stairway, and down a hall. We stopped beside a door and Eko cupped his hand around my ear. Speaking quickly, he explained that we were about to meet with a class of ninth-grade girls. I wasn't supposed to talk about politics or religion. "The kids are learning English," he said. "Just spend a few minutes talking about America, then answer their questions."

The headmaster opened the door and directed us to the front of the classroom. Sitting before twenty young ladies donned in head scarves and colorful blouses, I told them why I was traveling around the world and a bit about America—without referencing anything remotely controversial, which is actually quite hard. Then I asked if they had any questions.

The room burst into giggles, then quickly grew silent. After several seconds, one of the girls asked if we could be Facebook friends.

I looked at Eko for guidance and he nodded. "Sure," I said. "We can be friends."

Silence returned to the room. Then one of the girls asked if I'd ever met Justin Bieber.

"Nope," I said with a chuckle. "Have you?"

The room exploded in laughter. After a minute of silence, a hand in the back of the room slowly rose. I pointed to a shy-looking girl, and in broken English, she asked what I thought about hijabs.

I considered for a moment how to respond. I didn't want to offend anyone. These people had invited me into their religious school and shown me hospitality.

"They're beautiful," I said with a smile. A few girls blushed and several looked at the floor. "But I don't think girls should be forced to wear them against their will."

I was surprised to see most of the girls react with restrained smiles. Even the teacher nodded affirmatively. After posing for photos with the students, Eko and I said goodbye. The headmaster brought us back down to the courtyard and shook our hands.

"As-salamu alaykum," he said, the customary Muslim greeting meaning, "The peace be upon you."

Eko and I repeated the phrase, then got onto his motorbike. As we drove out of the courtyard and underneath the crescent moon, hundreds of children stood around the railing of the three-story building, shouting and waving. All I could do was smile and wave back.

From Eko's village, we traveled west to Yogyakarta. Several days later, we took an overnight train to Probolingo, another train to Jember, then caught motorbike taxis to Pantai Watu Ulo, a fishing village on the southern coast of East Java.

While there, a local fisherman and his six-year-old son, Kiki, befriended me, and one night they invited me to their home in Jember. It sounded like an adventure, and honestly, a good opportunity to do something without Eko. Part of the reason I traveled was to start over, but with Eko constantly by my side, my past felt unavoidable, strapped around me like my backpack.

With excitement—and a tinge of relief—I hopped on the fisherman's motorbike with his son and we raced away from the village. Soon after arriving at his house, a group of children from the neighborhood swarmed me and started shouting. I couldn't know for sure what they said, but it seemed they wanted me to dance like Michael Jackson. So I did what any person in my position would do. I pulled out my only MJ move—a little something my high school physics teacher, Mr. Price, taught me, called the moonwalk.

As I magically slid across the concrete floor while attempting to beatbox "Thriller," the kids fell to the ground and laughed hysterically. I felt my face flush red. Then everyone's attention shifted to the doorway.

I looked up and saw Kiki walk into the room carrying a small cage. Inside, a baby monkey sat with his hand in his mouth. I later found out the monkey fell from his mother's arms in the fishing village, and Kiki's dad brought it home to keep as a pet.

The kids raced to the cage and poked their fingers inside, trying to pet the animal. The monkey scurried to the corner and hugged his arms around his legs. My heart dropped, and instinctively, I rushed to the cage. But then I stepped back.

Though I wanted to tell the kids to leave him alone or even open the cage and let him escape, I knew there was little I could do. The kids couldn't understand a word I spoke, and without anyone to care for him in the wild, he would likely get injured or starve to death.

So I just stood there and watched.

THE NEXT MORNING, EKO AND I CAUGHT MOTORBIKE TAXIS TO THE train station in Jember, then we purchased tickets back to Probolingo through Banyuwangi, the port city to Bali. Part of me wondered if it was time to head out on my own. Eko mentioned returning to his village, and I wanted to go back to Bali and learn how to surf. After telling Eko my plans, he gave me directions to Bali.

The train was largely empty, so we each took a row to ourselves. Once the train pulled out of the station, I stretched out my legs, leaned my head on a seat cushion, and closed my eyes. At first my mind went blank, tired from the flurry of traveling.

Then I began thinking about whether I really could leave Eko behind. On the one hand, I didn't want to abandon my friend and make him feel any more alone than I imagined he already felt. I could tell the isolation of living in Indonesia wore on him. In fact, the empathy I felt toward him in DC had only increased. And just like back then, I felt a responsibility to protect him.

Yet on the other hand, I'd grown tired of traveling together. As hard as it was to admit, I distrusted Eko, and even more troubling, I realized that I felt constantly on guard around him, like he might do something unpredictable.

Then it hit me—the memory I'd tried to ignore for years, the reason Eko stopped living with my roommates and me in DC. He'd done something behind my back that really hurt me, something I never imagined a friend could do. But instead of confronting him, I pretended it hadn't happened, even though we both knew it had.

Every time the memory entered my mind over the years, I quickly pushed it away. But this time, for some reason, it wouldn't budge. I tried to force it out of my brain, but it kept growing and growing like a cancer, until it was all around and within me, consuming everything.

That's when I knew I needed to leave. I couldn't be around someone who had violated my trust so badly. For years I minimized what Eko did to me. I told myself it wasn't a big deal or maybe hadn't even happened. But I couldn't lie to myself anymore. I didn't want to lie to myself.

That didn't mean I wanted to deal with it. If anything, I wanted to run from my past even faster.

So I did.

At the next stop, I picked up my backpack, waved goodbye to Eko, and stepped off the train. Standing on the platform, I watched the string of railroad cars pull away from the station and slip around a bend, leaving me alone.

3

MONSOON NEARING

An airy drizzle fell as I sat on the bow of a ferry making its way across the Bali Strait. Several Indonesians sat around me, puffing cigarettes and chatting, their words radio static to my ears. Reclining uncomfortably on a plastic chair, I locked my eyes on the horizon and watched the sky dim to gray as dark clouds shrouded the sun.

I felt relieved to get away from Eko and finally be on my own. Over the past three weeks, he had essentially acted as my guide, deciding everything for me—where to go and what to do, where to sleep and what to eat. While it helped me acclimate to a foreign country, it made traveling too easy.

Throughout my life I had played the part of the little brother. I suppose it was the natural result of having two older brothers who never hesitated to box me into that role. If they weren't picking on me, they were still treating me as their kid brother.

This dynamic grew so familiar, it melded into my identity. Even after graduating from college and moving to DC, I fell into this role with friends—always seeking advice, always doing what others wanted, always following the lead.

Recently, though, the role no longer fit. While I didn't always see myself as a man, I wanted to grow into that role. So in planning this trip, I built in a lot of alone time. I didn't want to always travel with other people, like Eko, who because of their familiarity with an area, naturally took control. I wanted to head out on my own with no one to guide me. I wanted to determine everything for myself.

I had this nagging sense that facing the unexpected without a guide, or a step-by-step protocol, or even a general plan, was necessary for my growth. Any husband or father must have the confidence and know-how to lead and improvise and take responsibility, even on unfamiliar and unmapped roads. And I desired those roles for my future. I wanted to be the sort of man my future wife, children, and friends admired and respected—not because I conformed to our culture's macho version of masculinity with its farting and football and impenetrable shell, but because I embodied a strong and courageous and principled masculinity.

This trip, then, was a test. Could I make it on my own? Could I take care of myself without anyone's help? Could I adventure alone without hesitation? Could I take the lead instead of letting circumstance control me?

Turning my eyes from the horizon, I noticed a boy sitting on his mother's lap. He peeked over her shoulder and began watching me. His eyes hung on my face, scrutinizing my every move.

I flashed a grin and said, "Hello."

An astonished smile broke out on the boy's face and he sheepishly hid behind his mother. Startled by my voice, she turned around and looked me up and down.

"What you doin'?" she asked, tilting her head.

I sprang up in my chair. "Traveling to Kuta."

Her face came to life, morphing from suspicion to elation. "You must take shuttle with my nephew, Dewa."

"Okay...."

"He drives tourist van from Gilimanuk to Kuta. He is cheapest. Safest too."

I nodded, mulling over her suggestion. I did need a ride to Kuta and had little reason to doubt this woman's honesty. "Where can I find him?"

"When ferry docks," she said, struggling to pronounce the words, "cross street to parking lot." She paused for a few seconds, scrunching her face. "His van say, 'Dewa's Shuttle.' You see him. I promise."

"Sounds simple enough."

"Oh," the woman shouted, grabbing my shoulder and pulling me toward her. "And tell him Asmawati sent you."

"Asmawati?"

"Yes. That is me. Asmawati."

"Okay. I'll tell him Asmawati sent me. Thank you."

I ruffled the boy's hair, then walked to the railing and looked down. The sea fought against the ferry, riling a mosh pit of plastic bags, cigarette packages, and Styrofoam cups. As we neared Bali, I followed a stream of people to the lower bow and waited for the castle-like doors to drop over the water. Once ashore, I followed Asmawati's directions and quickly found the van.

I handed the driver 50,000 rupiah, the equivalent of $5.50. "Your aunt sent me."

He scrunched his forehead. "Aunt?"

"Yeah. Asmawati."

"Damn commission," he said under his breath. With a forced smile, he took my cash. "Get in van, we go now."

Inside the van, I squeezed past three rows of locals and found an empty seat in the back. Then I tried to fall asleep.

THREE HOURS LATER, WE ARRIVED IN THE COASTAL CITY OF KUTA. I stepped out of the van and into the dark, humid evening. A drizzle pattered the streets and a breeze brushed against my hair, bringing with it the brackish smell of the sea. While I contemplated whether to take a taxicab or motorbike taxi, the drizzle transitioned into a light rain.

Looking to save cash, I approached a motorbike and asked the driver if he could take me to Kuta Beach. Dressed in a faded t-shirt, shabby shorts, and worn-out flip-flops, he looked like a beach bum.

"12,000 rupiah," he said.

The price sounded high. "6,000?"

He shook his head.

I thought for a moment. "9,000?"

"Okay."

"9,000?" I asked again, making sure he'd accepted my offer— a habit leftover from my contracts course in law school.

"Yeah yeah yeah," he said, waving his hand in a circle. "Monsoon nearing, let's go."

I hopped behind the driver, then grabbed his shoulder with one hand and the seat with my other hand. He popped the clutch and the bike darted onto the road. Weaving through traf-fic, headlights stabbed in every direction and high-pitched horns pierced my ears. I struggled to keep my body upright against the g-forces pulling at my backpack, trying to drag me onto the pavement.

Suddenly, the sky opened—unleashing barrels of water too heavy for the clouds to hold. Everything on my body was instantly soaked. My clothes. My backpack. Even my jacket.

"Drop me off at the McDonald's," I shouted. "The one by the beach."

Without slowing, the driver looked back at me. "I take you to very nice hotel. My brother is owner. He take care of you."

"I don't think so," I said, signaling with my hand for the driver to watch the road.

"Just look. No pressure."

I shook my head. "No thanks."

In defeat, the driver turned around. Then he accelerated the bike. Dangerously, almost recklessly, he veered into the middle of the road, between vehicles traveling in opposite directions, and raced in front of a bus. He pulled the same maneuver to pass a slow-moving car.

As the driver continued weaving through traffic and the rain continued pounding, I fought against every instinct to close my eyes. I wanted to own my decision. If I died in a motorcycle accident, I wanted to see it coming.

When we pulled up to the McDonald's, I jumped off the motorbike. Across the street, the beach looked abandoned. A river of rainwater rushed down the road.

I pulled out a 10,000 rupiah bill and handed it to the driver. "Keep the change."

The driver took the money and raised a peace sign, then raced away.

I jogged across the street and into the restaurant, my waterlogged shoes squishing with every step. Indonesian pop music blared from speakers in the ceiling and a group of teenagers eyed me with amusement. I spotted an empty table in the corner and sat down, then removed my drenched shoes, socks, fedora, and jacket, and unloaded my backpack. With my belongings slowly drying, I waited for the deluge to let up long enough to sneak outside and find somewhere to sleep for the night.

After thirty minutes, the storm still raged and my stomach roared to life. Seeing that I was conveniently located at McDonald's, I ordered a cheeseburger. It was the first familiar food I had eaten in three weeks—and I loved it. It tasted so good, I scarfed down a second one. Then I got in line for an ice cream cone.

"What flavor?" the employee standing behind the counter asked. Wearing a baggy uniform and an oversized hat with bleached blonde hair poking around its edges, he perfectly fit the role of disengaged twentysomething. His clear enunciation signaled a grasp of English.

"Vanilla," I said, handing him a bill and some change.

The guy grabbed the cash while staring at me with a cold expression. Then he extended his hand. "My name's Gunter."

I reached back and shook his hand. "Good to meet you, I'm Paul."

"You from America, Paul?"

"I am, Gunter. And as you can see, I didn't come prepared for your country's monsoons."

He looked past me and spotted my belongings scattered across a table. "I see," he said, nodding his head. "Most tourists don't." He placed the money into a cash register and punched a few buttons, moving slowly despite the growing line behind me.

"Do you know where I can find a place to stay around here?"

Gunter looked up from the register and pointed to his left. "A block that way. You'll find all sorts of guesthouses." He paused, as though stumbling upon an idea. "But…if you need somewhere to crash tonight, I've got a flat outside of town."

His offer surprised me and I didn't know what to think. Gunter must have noticed my reluctance because he snapped his tongue and said, "Don't worry, man. Just thought you'd be up for a good time."

"I think I'm fine with a guesthouse."

"You sure? You could take my bed."

I paused for a moment, not wanting to offend him with an outright rejection. "Yeah, I don't think so. I'm planning to surf in the morning so I really should stay nearby."

Gunter nodded like he didn't care, then turned around and fiddled with the ice cream machine. A few seconds later, he handed me a cone with a perfectly-formed tower of ice cream. "I get off in ten minutes," he said, almost as an afterthought. "I'd be happy to help you find a guesthouse."

I looked outside at the still-pouring rain, then at the table with all of my things. Then I looked back at Gunter. "Do you have a scooter?"

"Yep."

"Do you happen to have an extra jacket I could borrow to wrap around my backpack?"

"Nope." He paused. "But I have an idea." He slipped away and came back with a black trash bag.

I returned to my table and, holding the ice cream cone with one hand, repacked my backpack with the other. Then I lifted the beast into the trash bag and tied the opening into a knot.

Once I finished the ice cream, I followed Gunter back into the storm, sat on the back of his motor scooter, and wrapped my arms around the trash bag. Gunter started the engine and we creeped down the street through pools of standing water.

At the first hotel, I ran inside to check the price. It was too expensive, so I returned outside and asked Gunter to keep driving. We went through the same routine twice more, but by the fourth time I lost patience and agreed to pay 200,000 rupiah.

I ran back to Gunter with my shoulders hunched forward and my head lowered in an attempt to dodge the rapid-fire rain. "I think I'm gonna stay here."

Gunter looked disappointed. "Really? You sure you don't wanna stay at my place? You'll have more fun."

I looked at the hotel and then quickly back at Gunter. I didn't care about offending him anymore. I just wanted to be alone. "Yeah. I'm alright by myself."

"If you have second thoughts," he said, tilting his head, "you know where to find me."

"Bye, Gunter," I said, waving as I turned and ran back to the hotel.

I paid for one night, confident I could find somewhere cheaper in the morning, then hurried to my room. Although small, it had a queen-sized bed with a wooden bed frame and a ceiling fan. After unpacking my backpack and hanging my clothes on the furniture to dry, I went back outside in search of an internet café. I hadn't gone online for days.

A steady rain still fell, but at least the monsoon had passed. I jogged down the street a few blocks until I found a convenience store with a neon "Internet" sign in the window. An attendant sat behind the counter smoking while watching me suspiciously.

At a makeshift table in front of a flickering monitor, I pushed aside a pile of cigarette butts and pulled up my email. Other than a bunch of spam and an email from my parents, I found two messages from Alissa. I deleted the junk mail first, then read and responded to my parents' email—delaying gratification as long as possible to heighten the already-brimming anticipation.

Then I read Alissa's emails, once quickly, then slowly a second time, imagining her speaking every word. It drove me crazy. I spent thirty minutes crafting a response, updating her on my travels and telling her I returned to Bali because I wanted to surf. Then I paid the attendant 3,000 rupiah and headed back outside.

Only a light rain fell and it seemed oddly quiet—the aftershock of a jarring monsoon on a beach town. I took my time walking to the hotel, looking at each storefront and passing the occasional backpacker or surfer. It felt nice to be alone, and more importantly, far from everything familiar.

At one point, muddy water flooded the street, so I rolled up my pant legs and immersed my feet into the puddle. Before crossing through, I heard a noise and looked up. A woman on a motor scooter turned from a cross street and started heading straight for me. She looked middle-aged, around thirty-five or so, and a blue poncho draped her slender body. As she passed, she glanced to the side and we made eye contact.

Quickly, she pulled a sharp U-turn, swerved in front of me, and stopped in my path. For a few seconds we looked at each other, neither of us uttering a sound. Then her mouth moved.

"What?" I said, shaking my head.

She spoke again, but I still couldn't make out her words.

"I can't hear you."

Her face grew frustrated and she repeated herself again, this time raising her voice.

I shook my head and said, "I'm sorry." I reached into my pocket and felt loose change. I didn't have much, but I considered offering it to her.

In a sudden movement, she jerked herself off the scooter, stepped forward, and thrust her face close to mine. Her breath, rotten like sulfur, filled my nostrils. "You wanna *do* me?"

Her words slammed into me, sucking the air from my lungs. I tried to turn, but I couldn't. My legs wouldn't move and I couldn't look away. She looked sad yet determined. Confident yet distant. And it scared me, because somewhere inside, I felt transported back in time to that awful night as a fourteen-year-old.

As I stared into her dark brown eyes, adrenaline surged through my body and my mind raced through the next hour.

Grabbing her arm and leading her to my room. Removing our clothes and caressing her body. Everything changing in the blink of an eye, the beat of a heart. The weight of regret as her head rested on my chest, rising and falling with each suffocating breath.

Then, like waking from a nightmare, I remembered: I'm not a child anymore. I'm a man. Now I have the strength to say no. Now I have the courage to turn and leave. And no one can stop me.

Tightening my jaw, I shook my head. Anger shot through the woman's face and her eyes narrowed. As she stared at me, the silence grew deafening—no rain, no traffic, no noise.

"No," I finally said.

Her eyes remained locked, as though she could force me to do whatever she wanted. But she couldn't. Nobody could.

"No," I repeated, raising my voice.

A moment later, she looked to the ground.

I stepped past the woman and crossed through the flooded street onto the drying sidewalk. Behind, an engine started and quickly faded until it made no sound at all.

4

SURFING IN BALI

Waves rolled in from beyond the horizon, breaking on the shore with a punch. Excited shouts burst from children frolicking on the beach and bodysurfing. Further out, a line of surfers sat on surfboards, rising and falling with the ocean. Even further still, sailboats floated atop the light blue water, their white sails filled with the breeze. And beyond them, the sun descended toward the Indian Ocean.

Along with a crowd scattered across Kuta Beach, I sat on the white sand and watched the sunset. What really interested me, though, were the surfers.

For a time in high school I dreamed of learning to surf. I loved the idea of gliding across a wave on a six-foot board, powered by nothing more than the force of gravity. The adventure appealed to a longing within.

Although I eagerly followed the rules while growing up, by the time I became a teenager, I no longer liked that role. I wanted more from life—to embrace risks and drift outside the boundaries. Surfing symbolized a break from the predictable, freedom from the constraints of my rigid personality. Because the guys who surfed, guys like Jeremy and his buddies, were the furthest thing from cautious and conventional. And from me.

They dressed in baggy clothes from local skate shops; mine came from the mall. They never combed their hair; I styled mine every morning. They showed up at school late after crawling out of bed; I woke up early and arrived on time. They showered once a week; I bathed daily. They ditched class; I only snuck off campus once or twice. They drank alcohol and smoked pot; I avoided both.

Sometimes I sat near them in the cafeteria to overhear their stories—waking before sunrise, driving west through the forested hills of the Coastal Range, squeezing into a wetsuit and plunging into the near-freezing water of the Pacific, and then riding waves until sunset. While I often spent weekends alone, chatting with online friends or playing video games, they relished life, enjoying the ocean's beauty and having fun together. Hearing their adventures left me jealous, because I could never be like them.

That didn't keep me from daydreaming. During class, I imagined drifting in the ocean beside them, gripping our boards as we floated over waves, until spotting a monster rising from the sea and riding it to shore.

For years I mourned my failure to befriend those guys. I regretted never getting into the ocean alongside them and surfing. If only I had reached out, if only I had tried, perhaps I could have broken free and enjoyed life more as a teenager.

Sitting on Kuta Beach watching the sun touch the horizon, I decided now was the time to learn to surf. With an hour of daylight, I figured I had plenty of time to get in the water and pick up the basics. So I wandered down the beach, looking for the twentysomething beach bum who had stopped me earlier and offered lessons.

"My name's Bobby," he had said in a Balinese accent. "Find me when you need me. I'm here all day every day."

The beaches in Bali were filled with guys like Bobby, locals in their twenties or thirties or even forties who took on western names and lived on the beach, teaching tourists to surf or providing companionship to women traveling solo.

I found Bobby sitting underneath a palm tree with some friends, a cigarette dangling from his mouth. He had long scraggly hair and dark brown skin, and he wore nothing but board shorts that sagged low on his waist, exposing his butt-crack.

"Bobby," I said, walking toward him. "You still have time to give me a lesson?"

A smile animated his face, displaying large white teeth. "Absolutely." He hopped to his feet and grabbed a blue surfboard leaning against the palm tree. Then he flicked his cigarette onto the sand. "Let's go," he said, handing me the surfboard while walking past me.

His friends nodded. "Get psyched," one of them shouted.

"Can I leave my stuff here?"

One of them nodded. "Of course."

I took off my shirt and flip-flops and set them on the sand, underneath the palm tree. Then I quickly pulled my wallet out of my pocket and hid it underneath my shirt. I glanced at the guys. Each of them nodded.

Hesitating, I considered calling off the lesson and returning the next day without my wallet. But it was just another excuse. For years I invented them, justifications to avoid risks.

I caught up with Bobby and, as we approached the ocean, he ran through the basics of surfing. Using exaggerated hand motions and stopping to demonstrate, he explained how to paddle, push through the wave break, judge the timing of waves, and finally, stand on the board. When we reached the shore, I felt confident I'd be thrashing waves in no time.

With a smirk, I lodged the board between my arm and body, and walked into the ocean.

The next hour felt like a fight—with the current, the board, my body, the wind, and especially the waves. Even as I struggled to keep my head above water or remain balanced on the board, the waves refused to let up.

All the while, Bobby stood on the shore, resting his hands on his waist and shouting instructions. Occasionally, he slogged into the water to clarify a point or correct my form, but I was on my own. If I wanted to surf, I had to keep fighting.

As darkness descended, I finally stood on the board and rode a wave. Then I did it again. And again. And again. Each time, Bobby hollered from the shore and thrust his fist into the air.

Eventually I paddled back toward shore. Digging my hands into the water and kicking my feet, I felt overjoyed. Not only had I learned to surf, I tasted the thrill of riding across a wave with the wind blowing through my hair.

"Dude," Bobby shouted. "You killed it."

I picked up the board and walked toward him, dripping a trail of water behind me. "That was awesome," I said, brushing my hand through my hair. "It's pretty exhausting too."

He laughed. "For sure. You'll be pro soon enough."

We made our way back to the palm tree, where Bobby's friends waited with a glass bottle of Fanta. One of them tossed it at me and, as it twisted in my direction, I snatched it out of the air. Then in one motion, I unscrewed the cap and chugged it.

"Thanks, man," I said, nodding at Bobby. "How much do I owe you guys?"

Bobby shrugged, his eyes locked on a girl in a bikini walking past us. "Whatever you want, champ."

I rummaged through my things, looking for my wallet—but I didn't see it. Then it fell out of a fold in my shirt and landed in the sand. Picking it up, I caught a glance from one of the beach bums. He was smirking, probably amused by the brief look of panic on my face. I pulled out a few paper bills and handed them to Bobby.

"Thanks a lot," I said.

"No worries, dude." He slipped the money into his pocket. "See you in the ocean."

I said goodbye to Bobby and his friends, then meandered across the beach and onto the main street through town, a narrow road lined with restaurants, shops, and guesthouses. Scooters and cars squeezed past one another, and swarms of tourists and locals spilled over the sidewalks.

My place was a few blocks away—different from where I stayed during the monsoon. The sign in front described it as a guesthouse, but from the street it looked like a shack. Down a narrow walkway, it opened to a lush garden overflowing with flowers and large-leafed trees that provided shade for a koi pond. Six rooms surrounded the garden, each with its own front patio. It was ideal for budget travelers like me.

As I walked through the garden, I saw a guy around my age reclining on the patio next to mine, flipping through a surf magazine. Before going inside, I introduced myself. His name was Tom, and he was from England. With blond hair and a solid build, I figured he could have passed for Daniel Craig's younger brother.

"You comin' back from surfing?" he asked in a British accent.

"Yup," I said, sitting on the ledge of my patio. "Just finished my first lesson."

Tom set the magazine down and turned toward me. "It went alright?"

"I think I'm hooked."

"So am I," he said with a chuckle. "Are you up for catching some waves tomorrow?"

"Absolutely."

"Great." Tom stood and hopped off his patio. Wearing a faded blue t-shirt and tan chino shorts, he looked like he was headed out for the night. "You have a chance to meet our Canadian neighbors, Eric and Brittany?"

"Yeah, they're cool."

I met Eric and Brittany earlier in the day when I checked into my room. Later, we ate lunch across the street. They were in their early twenties and hailed from small towns in Canada. Eric was laid-back and fun, the sort of guy I could see as a fraternity social chair. He had a shaved head and stood a bit taller than me.

Brittany was cute, petite, and spunky. Light brown hair fell over her shoulders and her face drew interest from every guy who laid eyes on her. In an eerie way, she looked like a girl I liked in high school but never worked up the courage to ask out. I found her both interesting and attractive. Not that it mattered now. I suspected Eric and Brittany were dating, and, of course, I wouldn't risk my relationship with Alissa. At least I didn't think so.

"We're heading to Bingin Beach tomorrow morning," Tom said. "It's supposed to be perfect for beginners, but not as crowded as Kuta. You should join us."

"Sweet. I'd love to."

"Awesome." Tom began walking down the path, out of the garden, but before rounding a corner, he looked back. "See you bright and early."

"Thanks," I shouted.

For the rest of the night, I couldn't stop thinking about surfing. And seeing Brittany again.

THE NEXT MORNING, I HOPPED ON THE BACK OF TOM'S SCOOTER AND we drove to a surf shop nearby. After renting a board, I set it beside his in the two-fingered rack extending from the left side of his scooter—it seemed every bike in Bali had a surf rack— then we circled back to our guesthouse.

Eric and Brittany were waiting for us on a motor scooter. I made eye contact with Brittany and felt my heart leap.

"You mates ready?" Tom said, revving his scooter.

Eric nodded enthusiastically. "You better believe it."

Brittany yawned from the back. "Yeah, I guess we'll come along...seeing we've got nothing better to do."

"Trust me, you guys will love this place," Tom said. "The waves are sick."

As Tom revved the engine again, a seed of uncertainty sprouted in my mind. Maybe I wasn't ready for "sick" waves. Maybe I needed to stay behind and surf the small ones at Kuta Beach. I didn't want to humiliate myself, especially in front of people I'd only just met.

Before I had a chance to do anything about it, Tom took off. With Eric and Brittany towing close behind, we wound through the narrow streets of Kuta and onto a two-lane highway running south along the coastline. Other than clouds on the horizon, the sky was a mirror image of the ocean.

Gripping the seat, I leaned back and closed my eyes. Warm air rushed against my face, scattering my hair like a wind wheel. For the first time since beginning my journey, I felt free from the busyness of my life back home, liberated from the franticness of studying and work and trying to get ahead. It was refreshing, like a drink of water after a long run.

I didn't need to worry about the daily grind. I didn't need to worry about falling behind. I could simply enjoy life, the whimsy and joy of every moment. That meant pushing against discomfort. Embracing uncertainty. Not waiting to live life—not holding off until the precise moment everything felt right. But living life right now.

Suddenly, I heard two high-pitched yelps. I opened my eyes and saw Eric and Brittany cruising inches beside us. They stared at me pie-eyed, as though witnessing the strangest sight of their lives.

With my body arched back and my hair fluttering, I'm sure I looked like a wild man. And I loved that idea—that they thought of me as someone other than who I'd always been. The "good kid." The "evangelical Christian." The "conservative Republican." Not that faith and politics aren't important. I just didn't want to wear them on my sleeve like plastic pins. Politics isn't a business card, and faith isn't a bumper sticker—nor should it simply be a set of habits and routines.

I wanted a faith that liberated. Not in a crazy, out of control way. But a faith unleashed to pursue God's unique design for my life. And I suspected that didn't look like the square, suit-wearing politico or the prude, straight-laced teenager. I was tired of playing those parts, exhausted from keeping up the image.

"You alright?" Brittany shouted, her voice muffled by the wind.

"Yeah," I said, trying to keep from cracking up. "I'm...finding my happy place."

Both Eric and Brittany started laughing, and after struggling to maintain my pose, I broke down and laughed with them.

Tom glanced behind his shoulder and rolled his eyes. "Bloody wankers."

That only made us laugh harder until Tom raced in front of Eric and Brittany, and we continued south another twenty miles. By the time we arrived at Bingin Beach, clouds masked the landscape and large drops of water sprinkled from the sky, falling around us like scattershot. Holding our surfboards above our heads to shield us from the rain, we sprinted from our scooters to a shack overlooking the ocean.

As soon as we reached cover, the heavens opened. The four of us took seats around a plastic table and watched rain collide with the ocean and waves smash against the beach. Everyone looked discouraged, especially Tom. He'd promised a great expe-rience, and not only was this place deserted, a sign it probably wasn't too impressive, but the flash monsoon prevented us from getting in the water. I tried not to show my relief.

"Anyone got a story?" I asked after a while.

"A story?" Brittany said, shifting her eyes to me. "What is this, show and tell?"

I chuckled. "Nope, but it does look like we'll be stuck here for a bit…." I waited to see if anyone would volunteer, but every-one's eyes remained glued to the ocean. "I guess that'd be a no."

"If you're so eager," Brittany said, leaving the sentence unfin-ished. She flashed a smirk, and I sensed she was testing me.

Tom nodded. "Yeah, Paul. Let's hear your best Bali story."

"Alright, alright," I said, already regretting the idea. "Well, when I arrived a few weeks ago, a friend and I traveled around the island, exploring a different city every day."

"Sweet," Eric said, speaking up for the first time since we got to the beach. His eyes looked tired.

"Yeah, it was great. Late one afternoon we stopped at Amed, a town on the north shore with a beautiful beach covered in black rocks. No surfing, obviously, but I'd heard the snorkeling was great. So I grabbed my mask and snorkel and headed into the ocean. The water was actually pretty rough and right away I felt coral under my feet—the sharp and jagged kind that'll eat you up with one wrong move. But, of course, I wanted to snorkel. So I swam through the water, careful not to skin myself in the process."

"Oh my," Brittany said softly.

"Yeah," I said, holding eye contact with her, a rush of adrenaline following. "But I maneuvered through the maze and swam past the waves until the ocean floor dropped. When I put my face in the water, I knew it'd been worth it—a thousand fish in a hundred colors spiraled below me. Barracudas. Bluefin trevally. Mahi-mahi. Ruby snappers. It was amazing. Not to mention the coral heads rising from the sea floor—a city of reds and oranges and yellows."

"Yeah, mate," Tom said. He looked at me proudly. "Good work."

"I thought so too," I said, followed by a nervous chuckle. "After a while, I popped my head above the water and looked toward shore."

"What'd you see?" Brittany asked. Her foot tapped like a drum.

"The tide had gone out." Everyone let out a moan. "A good twenty yards of coral stood between me and the shore—and the waves, they were only getting worse." I looked at the ocean thrashing at the beach, then back at them. "I was freaking out, afraid I'd shred a foot or smash my head if I tried to make it in."

"So what'd you do?" Eric asked.

"I only had one choice—get to shore. Otherwise I was stuck in the ocean for the night. So I found a spot where the waves weren't as bad, then began climbing over coral heads. Every few seconds, I grabbed whatever was in sight and braced for a wave to smash my back. One time, I lost my balance and nearly banged my knee, and another time, I slipped and almost fell backwards—if a wave had hit at that exact moment, my ankle would've snapped."

"Mother Mary," Tom said.

"After each wave, I scrambled forward another few feet, and slowly but surely, I worked my way across the coral until I finally reached the shore. I fell onto the black rocks and thanked God. It could've been *really* bad."

"That's crazy," Brittany said. Her face looked flush, like she'd been holding her breath, and I knew I passed her test.

"That's a great story," Tom said, standing and resting a foot on his chair. He leaned his elbow on his knee and his chin on his fist.

"He's getting serious," Brittany said with a laugh, shifting her eyes onto Tom.

Eric looked amused. "Like Rodin's statue."

"Just gettin' ready to entertain," Tom said, stretching his arms behind his head and taking two rapid breaths. "I've got to one-up Paul."

"Alright," I said, shaking my head and chuckling. "Let's hear it."

"A couple weeks ago," Tom began, eyeing each of us before continuing, "I drove down the coast to Pedang Pedang, a popular beach for pro surfers. Of course I only intended to watch, but after an hour, I had to get in the water."

"Very wise," Brittany said.

"I paddled out a couple hundred yards until I reached a group of surfers. Then after passing on several huge waves, I spotted one I thought I could handle. As it approached, I turned towards the shore, and in no time, I was on top of that beast. But right as I stood up, the front of my board dipped underwater."

"No way," Eric said, appearing to enjoy the prospect of Tom wiping out.

"Yup—I barreled forward into the massive wave. That thing destroyed me—flipping me around, pulling me in every direction. I held my breath until I started blacking out, then kicked like crazy. When I finally surfaced, I gasped for air, climbed onto my board, then looked around. And I kid you not, I didn't see another surfer anywhere."

"Remind me again why we followed you out here," Brittany said under her breath.

"I wanted to keep surfing, but I also knew I was in a sketchy situation—I had no idea where I was. So I decided to paddle back to shore. I tried catching a few waves on the way in, but didn't have much luck."

"Maybe because you'd just had a near-death experience," Eric said.

"Once I reached shore," Tom continued, "I quickly realized I was on another beach, separated from Pedang Pedang by a bunch of bloody rocks. I didn't feel like getting back into the water, so I found the highway and headed north—barefoot, shirtless, hauling my board on my shoulders."

"Comforting," Brittany said. "So what happened?"

"Some chick eventually picked me up and took me back to Pedang. Then I hopped on my scooter and followed her to Kuta. We ended up getting drinks and having a good time."

"Insane," I said, looking at the waves slamming onto the beach. Clouds of mist exploded, then dissipated into the wind. It wasn't so much that Tom almost lost his life surfing, but how he got himself into that situation to begin with, then turned it into a date.

Tom shrugged. "Just making lemonade."

"Not any I wanna taste," Brittany said, crossing her legs and leaning forward. Her face looked concerned, like she was having second thoughts about surfing.

"How about you?" I asked, looking at Eric.

Glaring at the ocean, a smirk stretched across his face. "I first visited Bali a few years ago," he said, shifting his eyes onto us. "Me and some buddies wanted to party, so we came to Kuta and hit up the nightclubs every night."

"Nightclubs?" I asked.

Brittany laughed, then quickly grew quiet. "Wait, are you serious?"

"What do you mean?" As soon as the words left my mouth, I realized I'd announced my naiveté. Everyone knows Bali's a party island. Somehow it slipped my mind Kuta's the epicenter, where everyone comes to score and get wasted.

"Other than surfing, that's the only reason people come to Kuta," she said, confirming what I recalled hearing elsewhere. "Gosh, Paul, we really need to show you a good time."

"Anyway," Eric said loudly, redirecting attention to himself. "We spent every night going from club to club, staying out until early the next morning. On the second night, we noticed some of the same local girls. One of them caught my buddy's attention, and we teased him until he worked up the courage to buy her a drink. Somehow, despite the language barrier and cultural differences, they hit it off, and every night after, they partied together."

Brittany rolled her eyes. "Where's this going?"

"On the last night, my buddy brought the girl back to his hotel and, well, one thing led to another." He paused to laugh. "Needless to say, when he woke the next morning, he felt terrible. He had a girlfriend back home—"

"Guys are awful," Brittany said.

I coughed, "Not all of them."

"—and he knew he'd made a mistake. But he couldn't let it go. He had to blabber about how bad he felt and how his girlfriend would dump him if she found out. He actually started crying."

"Wow," Tom said, his eyes wide in disbelief.

"So the girl puts her arm around my buddy's shoulder, leans close to his ear, and whispers that she's sorry. Then she steps out of bed and starts screaming—'I'm not leaving until I get paid, and if you have a problem, you can talk with the guy standing outside your door.'"

"What...in...the...hell," Tom shouted, jumping out of his chair, then sitting back down. "She was a hooker?"

Eric nodded. "Yup."

"What'd he do?" I asked.

"He paid her and she took off," Eric said, the smirk returning to his face. "Easy peasy."

"How much?" Tom asked.

Eric chuckled. "Twenty bucks."

"Worst story ever," Brittany said.

"Fine," Eric said, rolling his eyes. "Let's hear your story."

"You want a story? How's this for a story," Brittany said, firing the words out of her mouth. "One morning I woke up at the crack of dawn and hauled my ass thirty minutes south to a beach some British punk promised would blow my mind. But when we got there, not only was it completely abandoned, but we were stuck in a monsoon. So we sat there for God knows how long trading exaggerated travel stories."

"Yikes," Eric said.

"Whatever." Brittany tossed her hair behind her shoulder and stared down at us. "Lighten up, boys. I was only kidding."

"On another note," I said, "why's everyone traveling?"

"Winter in Canada sucks," Brittany said.

"Someone's bitter," Tom said.

"Actually, Eric and I are in grad school, and it's our last spring break before graduation. So we decided to go all out, travel around Asia for a couple weeks."

"I quit my job," Tom said. "I'm through with the rat race." He leaned back, propped his feet onto the table, and rested his hands behind his head. "For the next six months, I'll be right here, learning to surf. Then I'm moving to Australia, where I'll open a surf school for disadvantaged kids."

I nodded my head. "That's cool." I paused briefly. "Honestly, I'm really impressed."

"How about you?" Brittany asked, lifting her chin toward me.

"I just finished law school and had a few months to kill. So instead of working, I decided to wander around the world for a while."

Brittany's jaw dropped. "You're a lawyer?"

"Not quite. I find out if I passed the bar exam in two days. If I did, *then* I'll be a lawyer."

"That's it," Eric said, pounding his fists against the table. "You're partying with us before you leave. And there's nothing you can do to stop it."

Tom jumped into the conversation and insisted on telling another surf story. By the time he finished, the rain still fell hard and we were all growing impatient. Brittany rested her feet on the table and her eyes looked drowsy. Eric didn't seem much better himself. Tom was the only one who looked like he wasn't falling asleep.

"What do you say, team?" Tom said. "Should we give it another thirty minutes?"

Brittany looked at him doubtfully. "Even if it lets up, I'm not getting in *that* water."

Eric yawned. "Same here. It's a death trap. I think we're heading back. We can try Kuta Beach tomorrow."

Tom looked at me and frowned. "You too, Paul?"

"Sorry, bud. This storm isn't letting up."

"Alright," he said, jumping to his feet. "Let's go."

We grabbed our surfboards, walked back into the rain, and drove to our guesthouse in Kuta, returning drenched and exhausted—without having stepped foot in the water.

The next morning, I woke to a persistent knock. I crawled out of bed and cracked open my door. It was Tom—ready to surf.

"Paul," he shouted, shifting from one leg to the other like an excited puppy. He grabbed the door and pulled it open as I lifted my hand to shield the light. "Get your trunks on. We're grabbing breakfast, then heading to the beach."

I looked at Tom confused, squinting my eyes. "Who *are* you?"

He laughed. "Paul," he shouted again. "Everyone's waiting for you. Hurry up."

I shut the door, ran to the bathroom, and quickly brushed my teeth, put in my contacts, and changed into board shorts. When I stepped outside, Tom was lounging on my patio, drumming his hands on his knees. Eric and Brittany stood in the garden, looking exhausted.

"Late night?" I said, eyeing Brittany.

"Every night's a late night with this guy," she said, nodding her head sideways.

"You better believe it," Eric said. "And your turn's coming soon." He pointed at me and winked.

I laughed uncomfortably. "Okay...."

Tom popped out of his chair. "Let's get breakfast."

We walked across the street and ate pork soup from a food cart. Then we grabbed our surfboards from the guesthouse and headed to Kuta Beach.

Although it was only eight o'clock, the beach was already packed. Swarms of kids, teenagers, and adults shuffled in and out of the water, carrying boogie boards and surfboards. Thousands more were sprawled across towels, sporting bikinis and Speedos. We struggled to make our way through the crowd without bumping people with our boards.

"This is a zoo," Brittany said.

"Which is why we tried a different beach yesterday," Tom said, veering to avoid a woman lying on a towel.

"Remind us again how that turned out," Eric said.

Tom dropped his head. "Come on, mate. It's still a bit raw."

Eric patted his back. "I'm only kidding, dude. You know we love you."

"Right," Brittany said with a chuckle. "Whatever would we do without our British monarch?"

At the edge of the ocean, we planted our boards into the sand. Eric, Brittany, and I looked at Tom and waited for his instructions. Nibbling his bottom lip and furrowing his brow, he examined the waves.

"Be careful out there," he finally said.

I scratched my head. "Why?"

Tom pointed at a wave. "Watch." As the wave fell forward, another wave crested close behind. "You see that?"

"Yeah," all three of us said in unison, our eyes hypnotized by the ocean.

"What is it, though?" I asked.

"Normally there's a gap between waves," Tom said. "But these are barreling in two and three at a time, one after the other. Some are even coming in diagonally," he said with a laugh.

"You sure it's not too dangerous?" I asked.

Tom nodded. "Yeah. It'll be fun."

"I'm not as brave as you guys," Brittany said, shaking her head. "I'm staying close to shore."

"Suit yourself," Tom said. Then he looked at Eric and me, and said, "I guess it's just the men."

The three of us picked up our boards and headed into the ocean. As I walked past Brittany, she smiled nervously and I waved goodbye. Once the water reached our waists, we lunged onto our boards and paddled to the first line of surfers. I sat on my board and watched the waves roll by, several people attempting to ride each one. Everyone quickly fell into the churning water.

Glancing at Tom and Eric, I suddenly felt afraid. It was only the second time I'd surfed, and I didn't feel prepared to handle anything other than small, predictable waves. And these waves were definitely not small or predictable. They were large and erratic. I'd made a mistake following them out there.

"You ready?" Tom asked, looking at us for a response.

"Yeah," Eric shouted, slapping his hand against his board. "Let's do this."

I nodded uneasily. "I guess so."

Tom must have sensed my apprehension, because he placed his hand on my shoulder. "You'll do great, Paul."

I tried to force a smile. "Thanks."

For the next thirty minutes, I stayed close to Tom and Eric, occasionally trying to catch a wave, but getting tossed around like a toy duck. The waves were too big and too rough, and they destroyed me. I eventually reached a point where I no longer cared about looking bad or keeping Tom and Eric happy. I just wanted to survive.

Gathering my courage, I split off and headed closer to shore. Even though the waves remained unpredictable, they were smaller, and I started standing on my board and surfing. After a while I grew convinced I'd mastered the sport. I envisioned moving to San Diego and hitting the waves with Jon Foreman and the rest of Switchfoot. They'd be so impressed with my moves they'd ask me to join them in the studio to record a new song. On our way there, we'd grab a bite to eat at their favorite Mexican joint.

My daydream ended in an instant. While riding a puny wave, I fell off my board. After getting thrashed around, I popped my head above the water and, gasping for air, saw another wave crashing on top of me—thrusting my surfboard straight at my face. I turned, but not quick enough.

The board smashed into my lip. Pain radiated from my mouth to my ear and my hand went to my face. I lowered it and saw blood, then slid my tongue over my teeth—none were missing, but my lip felt swollen.

It didn't seem like a serious injury, but the experience shattered my confidence and I didn't want to surf anymore. Heading toward shore, I spotted Brittany and she waved. Her mouth lifted into a slight smile as I walked out of the water.

"How'd it go?"

I tossed my surfboard next to her. "Not very well."

"Yeah?"

"Yeah. I got into a disagreement with my board and it sucker-punched my lip."

"Oh no." She jumped to her feet. "Let me see."

Brittany leaned toward me, then caressed the side of my lip with a finger. Her touch was delicate, and I struggled to keep from smiling. As she studied the wound, my eyes wandered from the ocean to her eyes. Mesmerized by the kaleidoscope of turquoise and greens, I didn't want to look away. But I knew I should.

After a few seconds, she stepped back. "It's not too bad. Just a little cut."

I exhaled. "That's a relief."

Brittany and I sat beside each other in front of my board. With our legs inches apart, I wondered if she was testing me again, this time to see if I'd make a move on her. Even if I hadn't been dating Alissa, I doubted I would have done anything. Some guys have an easy time hitting on girls—not me.

"Other than the slight mishap, how'd it go?" she asked.

I shook my head. "Pretty rough."

"Yeah, me too. I'm not sure surfing's my thing."

"Me neither."

For a minute, we didn't say anything. We just sat there and stared at the ocean. Then she asked if I saw Tom and Eric out there.

"We were together for a while, but I lost them when I came closer to shore."

Brittany raised her hand to her forehead and scanned the ocean. Then she lowered it and took a long, deep breath. A moment later, she glanced at my legs. Her eyes slowly rose to my chest, then to my face. I couldn't believe it, but she held her gaze, seemingly waiting for me to turn and face her. Adrenaline pumped through my body, and I wondered what would happen if I met her eyes.

"So, um, you and Eric," I said, my voice shaky, "how long have you been dating?"

Brittany laughed softly. "What makes you think we're dating?"

"Well," I stuttered. "You *are* traveling together."

"And?"

"I assumed…."

"You assumed wrong."

"Oh. Well, sorry. I just figured."

Brittany rubbed her temples with her middle and ring fingers. "No worries. It's just that we dated for a while last year, but now we're friends. At least that's how we try to keep it. But lately we've been acting like we're still together. I don't know." She shook her head and sighed. "Maybe it isn't over."

"Oh," I said, expressing more disappointment than intended. I wasn't sure why I felt bad, but I did. Had I just imagined things?

The next thing I knew, Brittany scuffled to her feet. "Oh God."

"What?" I said, jumping beside her. "What happened?"

"It's Eric," she said, her voice panicked. She pointed toward the ocean. "There's something wrong."

In the distance, I saw Tom and Eric hobbling through the ocean, the water chest-high. Every few seconds, a wave slammed into their backs and their surfboards rushed past them, halting at the end of their leashes. They each had an arm wrapped around the other's shoulder—Eric's free hand covered his face, and Tom held onto the leashes. Tom's face strained and his mouth moved like he was shouting, but against the roar of the ocean, his words didn't make a sound. Then I saw red pouring down Eric's face. And I knew it was blood.

"Stay here," I said. "I'll get help."

Before Brittany could respond, I took off down the beach, my feet struggling to balance on the loose sand and my lungs quickly growing strained by the thick heat. Dodging guys carrying surfboards and jumping over women lying on towels, I scoured the landscape for a lifeguard station. I ran for nearly five minutes before spotting one. When I reached it, my hands dropped to my knees and I struggled for a breath.

"Are you okay?" someone asked in broken English.

"Please help," I managed, raising my eyes. A Balinese man stood beside me with a red float strapped around his back. He looked like a lifeguard. "My friend's hurt. He needs help."

"Where?"

I straightened up and pointed down shore. "About a half-mile that way," I said, still catching my breath. "Please, call an ambulance."

The lifeguard shook his head. "Sorry, I can't help. There's a lifeguard station on the other side of your friend. You need to go there."

I stepped forward, my chest inches from the lifeguard, and stared into his eyes. "My friend needs your help *right now*...and you need to follow me."

For a moment, I didn't know what he'd say. But I didn't care. I'd do whatever it took to get him to help. I wouldn't back down.

The lifeguard's eyes dropped. "Okay."

"Thank you," I said, breathing a sigh of relief.

Immediately, I turned and sprinted down the beach, occasionally glancing over my shoulder to check on the lifeguard. At one point, he lifted the radio to his mouth, hopefully alerting an ambulance. Falling further behind, he huffed and coughed, perspiration flowing down his face. I didn't feel much better myself. My lungs burned, my feet were on fire, and my legs felt wobbly. My body pleaded with me to stop, or at least slow down, but everything within screamed for me to keep going, because Eric was in trouble and needed my help. So against the pain, I continued running.

"There they are," I shouted, pointing at a crowd in the distance.

Glancing back, I saw the lifeguard twenty yards behind me. He looked like he was about to stumble over his feet. I slowed down until he caught up.

"We're almost there," I said between breaths. "Just another minute."

He turned his head and heaved.

When we finally reached the crowd, I squeezed through the bodies to a tight opening in the center. I first saw Tom, pacing back and forth. He looked panicked, unsure what to do. Then I saw Brittany kneeling, whispering over and over, "Everything will be okay." Only then did I see Eric—sitting on the ground, his knees huddled against his chest, his head leaning forward, his hands covering his face, and blood dripping through his fingers, pooling on the sand.

There was nothing I could do. Only watch and wait.

Then I heard a siren far away. It grew louder, until it sounded like it was just behind me, then it stopped. The crowd stepped back and two paramedics in white shirts broke through, the lifeguard leading the way. The paramedics bent beside Eric and examined his blood-stained face, while the lifeguard waved his arms at the crowd, asking everyone to back away. Standing on both sides of Eric, the paramedics helped him to his feet and led him across the beach toward an ambulance parked on the street. Tom, Brittany, and I followed close behind, the three of us walking side by side in silence.

At the ambulance, the paramedics guided Eric into the back. Brittany climbed in after him. Turning, she faced Tom and me. Then we made eye contact. Her eyes looked puffy and tears trickled down her pink cheeks. I wanted to comfort her, to make her feel better. But I knew I couldn't.

Looking down, I broke eye contact and stared at the ground.

Tom placed his hand on my shoulder and squeezed tight. "Mate," he said, his voice unsteady. "Can you stay here, keep watch over our surfboards until we get back from the hospital?"

I looked at him and nodded. "Yeah. Of course. Anything."

He turned toward the ambulance and, before getting inside, looked back. "You're a good man, Paul. A really good man."

I shifted my eyes to Tom and felt a lump rise in my throat. "Thanks, Tom. I'll be waiting for you guys."

Tom stepped into the ambulance and pulled the doors shut. Then the vehicle drove away, disappearing over a hill. I slowly made my way back to the beach, where I collected our surfboards and sat under a palm tree.

Sitting on the white sand, I watched the sun lift into the sky. Underneath, a line of surfers floated atop the ocean, rising and falling with each passing wave. At first I didn't think about much. I just watched the surfers on the ocean's shifting surface.

Then I thought about Tom, Eric, and Brittany, and how surfing brought us together. Only days before, I just wanted to spend time alone learning to surf. Now I couldn't imagine Bali without them.

For so many years, I longed to escape the confines of my life. Projecting my angst onto a group of high school surfer kids, I thought they held the secret, the key to my freedom. I couldn't help wondering, all these years later, if what I really needed back then wasn't so much a new and adventurous sport, but a place to belong—friends who liked me and accepted me and counted me as one of their own.

5

WAITING AT THE BAR

With a bandage taped around his right eye and purple bruising on his cheek and nose, Eric looked like he either lost a fight or got beat up winning. It didn't seem to bother him, though, as he swung his visible eye from one end of the table to the other, recounting the story of nearly losing his eye. Tom, Brittany, and I sat across from him, scrunched together in an empty restaurant, listening in disbelief.

It turned out Eric's surfing accident could have been *much* worse. After falling off a wave, he popped above the water and his board smashed into his face—centimeters above his eye. Blood burst from the wound and a flap of skin slipped over his cornea, blocking his vision. As far as he knew at the time, he'd gone blind and would never see again. But an hour after arriving at the hospital, a doctor removed the skin covering his eye.

"I once was blind," Eric shouted, setting chopsticks on the table and wiping his mouth with a napkin. "But now I see." He tilted his chin to the ceiling and exhaled a guttural laugh. "And that's reason enough to party."

"Technically," Tom said, appearing to choose his words carefully. "With that bandage over your eye, you *are* half blind."

Eric laughed again, then reached across the table and punched Tom's shoulder.

"Ouch," Tom said.

"I love you, man. But my feelings for you the other day were not so warm. I literally thought my eye popped out of its socket, and you were pulling me back to shore, keeping me from finding it. Damn you."

I strained my face in pain. "I can't imagine. I'd totally understand if you weren't up for going out tonight."

"Paul," Eric shouted, flashing a playful grin. "Are you trying to use my injury to weasel out of partying?"

I cracked a smile and then forked some food into my mouth and swallowed. "No," I said. "You've got me all wrong."

"I think what Paul's trying to say is that you look like a carnival freak," Brittany said. "You're a one-eyed monster. The girls are going to bolt as soon as you step in the club."

"First, not true," Eric said, raising an index finger. "And second," he displayed another finger, "that's why I'm sporting these." He pulled a pair of black thick-rimmed sunglasses out of his breast pocket and placed them over his eyes. They sat crooked on his nose and the edge of the bandage protruded around the right lens.

Brittany snorted, suppressing a laugh. "I haven't seen those since the 1980s."

"You weren't alive in the '80s," Eric shot back. "And anyway, they're coming back in style."

Tom reached across the table and straightened the shades on Eric's face. "There you go. Now you look like Tom Cruise circa *Rain Man*."

Brittany grinned. "You do realize it's okay not to party for one night. None of us will hold it against you."

"Yeah, mate," Tom said delicately. "You're already loaded up on pain pills. Let's just chill; go back to the guesthouse and watch a film or something."

"Nope," Eric said.

"But you're wearing an eye patch, for God's sake," Brittany said.

Eric rolled his eye. "It's not an eye patch. It's a bandage. And anyway, it's Paul's last night in Bali. There's no way we're sending him off without a rager."

I laughed uncomfortably. He was right—early the next morning I flew to Thailand. But I had little interest in partying the night away.

"Can't argue with that," Tom said, reaching behind Brittany, grabbing my shoulder, and giving me a good shake.

Eric pumped his fist into the air. "Sweet," he said, singing the word with a vibrato.

"He's right," Brittany said, patting my thigh. "I can't believe you're leaving tomorrow."

"You're taking off two days later," I said, forcing a laugh. "And seriously, I have to wake up at four in the morning to find out if I passed the bar exam."

"You passed," Brittany said.

"Yeah, Paul," Tom said.

I shook my head. "You never know."

"Poppycock," Eric shouted. "Let's go."

Eric jumped from the table and stood over us. Following his lead, we tossed some paper bills next to our empty plates and left the restaurant.

Walking through the dark and crowded streets, I remained quiet as Tom, Eric, and Brittany traded laughs. All I could think about was whether I passed the bar exam.

It's the single most important test I would ever take. Without passing it, I couldn't practice law. All the hard work over the past three-and-a-half years would mean nothing if I failed.

Even after three months of intense preparation, there remained a chance I wouldn't pass. Every year there are smart people who graduate from top schools and study hard who nonetheless fail. I feared that might be me.

If I did fail, I would end my trip early, return to Oregon, and spend another three months preparing for the bar all over again. That prospect was enough to throw me into an obsessive cycle of what-ifs.

It came down to two possibilities: pass or fail. And in eight short hours, I would know my future.

As we climbed a wooden stairway to the club, bass from music inside throbbed against my body and a stream of college-aged guys bumped past us. The stairway opened onto an outdoor patio surrounded by trees. Dim yellow lights revealed a mist floating down from the sky. A crowd of local women stood by the doorway, wearing miniskirts and eyeing each guy walking inside. One girl approached a man and kissed him while two girls started flirting with a group of guys with cowboy hats.

We hurried past the women, trying to avoid their whistling. One of them clutched my arm and pulled me back. I jerked myself loose and continued through the doorway into the club.

Inside, hundreds of people packed two floors, contorting their bodies to a heavy beat and pounding shots, mixed drinks, and beer. Lights flashed from the ceiling and red, green, and blue spotlights appeared on the walls, disappearing seconds later. A pit covered in bubbly foam filled the center of the club. Women wearing only bras and panties slid inside, throwing foam at each other and screaming wildly. Crowds stood around the railing on the second floor, hollering at the action below. Across the room, sitting behind a table of electronic equipment on a raised stage, a DJ tossed his hands into the air as he faded from one techno beat to another.

We pushed through sweaty bodies until we found an opening near the bar. Tom made a beeline to the bartender, and Eric and Brittany began dancing to the music's thump. As I watched, I felt myself pulling back from everything around me.

DAYS AFTER MY THIRTEENTH BIRTHDAY, I WAS OFFERED A CIGARETTE for the first time. It was a chilly November afternoon, and my friend, Nicolas, and I were together. Since the day he walked into my third grade class, we were practically inseparable, in part because both of us were class clowns, yet we weren't trouble-makers.

Once we entered junior high (seventh grade), our friendship deepened as we navigated adolescence. We did everything together—ate lunch at school, talked on the phone at night, hung out at the mall on the weekends. Although I never told him, Nicolas was my best friend.

As the sun set that autumn afternoon, Nicolas and I walked through Cooks Butte Park, a forest near his house. We followed a dirt trail past towering Douglas firs toward a clearing overlooking the valley. We often went there because, hidden among trees and perched high above the city, it felt removed from our world—parents and siblings and homework and school. We were free to talk about everything there, from girls we liked and music we enjoyed, to thoughts about God. In a way, it was our hidden space. A respite from the shifting sands around us.

When we rounded a bend, we saw Ed, a friend of ours, along with three eighth-graders. They stood in a circle. We rarely saw other people there, not to mention someone we knew, and it seemed odd Ed would be with older kids. So we sped up to see what they were doing.

Then Ed lifted his hand to his mouth. Seconds later, what looked like fog drifted above his head and dispersed into the air, toward city lights in the distance. Everyone took a step back, and Nicolas and I squeezed beside Ed. The circle closed in tight. Without thinking, I looked at Ed's hand. Against the pebbled ground, I saw a cigarette—and my stomach dropped.

I knew this moment would one day arrive. Teachers drilled us about the dangers of smoking and resisting peer pressure. If I learned anything during my early years of public education, it was to "just say no." These messages were reinforced by my parents, who promised to give me $100 if I graduated high school without smoking or drinking. Even Adam, a thirty-two-year-old friend I met through my older brothers, did his part by making it look cool not to do drugs.

Without hesitation, Ed raised the cigarette to his mouth and inhaled. Then he turned his face toward the city and cracked his lips. Smoke wafted through gaps between his teeth as if bleeding from open wounds. There was something striking, even beautiful about the smoke as it curled in the air, then vanished into the graying sky.

Ed turned to Nicolas and asked if he wanted to try.

"Yeah," Nicolas said. Then he grabbed the cigarette.

I looked away just as Nicolas lifted it to his mouth. Seeing meant believing. After a few puffs, each followed by a cough, Ed took the cigarette and handed it to me.

I shook my head. "No thanks."

With those two words, that simple decision, I started down one path and Nicolas down another.

Tom RETURNED FROM THE BAR SPORTING A GRIN AND HOLDING FOUR glasses in his arms, pressed against his chest. "I hope everyone likes Singha."

Eric grabbed two beers and gave one to Brittany. "Anything with alcohol."

Tom handed me a glass, then signaled for everyone to gather near. We stepped closer, forming a tight circle.

"Toast to Paul," Tom shouted, raising his beer into the center of the group.

"Yeah," Eric and Brittany said, raising their beers.

I laughed. "For what? I haven't done anything."

"Mate," Tom said, "you're leaving tomorrow and we're gonna miss you."

I slowly nodded my head and said, "Oh."

"And," Brittany said, "we're getting a head start on celebrating."

"Celebrating?" I said.

She looked me up and down like I was crazy. "You passed the bar, doofus."

"Now you can sue people," Eric bellowed, lifting his glass toward my face.

I nudged his beer away and took a step back. "Not yet. I've still got seven hours until the results are posted online."

Brittany laughed. "Stop freaking out. You passed."

"Dude," Eric said, grabbing my arm and pulling me back into the circle. "Get your pint in here or we're toasting without you."

"Alright." I raised my beer and tapped it against their glasses. "To the three of you guys."

"To Paul," they shouted, lifting their beers into the air.

We all took a drink. I lowered my glass and Brittany followed. Tom and Eric continued chugging, apparently competing to see who could empty their glass first. Tom gave up with a quarter-pint remaining, but Eric kept drinking until his glass was dry. Then he opened his mouth and belched.

"Wonderful," Brittany said, rolling her eyes. "I think you made my insides rumble."

Eric stepped an inch from Brittany's face and began kicking his feet sporadically and popping his shoulders up and down. Brittany tossed her head back and laughed, then started imitating Eric. Tom chugged the rest of his beer, then let loose with an impressive robot.

"Come on, Paul," Brittany shouted, reaching her hand toward me.

I stepped forward and tried to dance, leaning from side to side and snapping my fingers to the beat of the music.

"He's definitely a lawyer," Eric said. "He might as well slip on one of those curly grey wigs."

Tom laughed. "I think those things sparked the American Rebellion."

"Seriously, Paul," Brittany said. "You need to loosen up."

I chuckled uncomfortably. "What do you mean? I'm having a good time."

The truth is, I felt miserable. As hard as I tried, I couldn't loosen up and have fun. So I gradually made my way to the bar. From there, I watched my friends drink and dance, and waited for the night to end.

SEVERAL MONTHS AFTER NICOLAS SMOKED A CIGARETTE AT THE lookout point, I noticed a new poster on his bedroom wall. It was a green marijuana leaf against black velvet.

"Why'd you get that?" I asked, pointing to the poster.

"Because it's cool," he said, glancing at me as though I wouldn't understand.

I turned from the poster and looked at him. "No, it's not."

He chuckled softly and shook his head. "Oh, Paul. You're still such a do-gooder."

Up to that point, I had tried to ignore the increasing divide between Nicolas and me. While he occasionally smoked and drank, everyone else did too. I saw no reason why it had to pull us apart. But as I stared at him, I could no longer deny reality. Nicolas had changed and our friendship had, too.

By the first day of eighth grade, I no longer hung out with Nicolas...or any of my friends, for that matter. Not because I didn't like them anymore. But because they grew tired of me watching while they had fun.

SWEAT GLISTENED ON BRITTANY'S FACE AND DRIPPED DOWN HER neck, dampening her shirt. Holding a beer in one hand, she grabbed my shoulder with her other hand and pulled me toward her.

"You doin' alright?" she asked, her voice hoarse from shouting over the past two hours.

I nodded. "Yeah. I'm fine. The music's just kinda loud for me. Doesn't it hurt your ears?"

She looked at me skeptically. "Have you ever been to a club?"

"Not like this one," I said, followed by a laugh. "But yeah, I'm doing okay."

"So why aren't you chilling with us?"

I leaned close to Brittany and whispered into her ear. "I'm not sure. I've got a lot on my mind, I guess."

"I see. Well, I wish you could set everything aside and at least try to have a good time."

I forced a smile and shrugged. "Sorry. Maybe next time."

Brittany shook her head dismissively. "There won't be a next time. And you know it."

Then she turned and walked back to Tom and Eric, who were taking pictures of one another doing crazy dance moves. The three of them bunched together and Eric held out the camera, a flash following soon after. Looking at the camera screen, they broke into laughter. Then Tom stopped a waitress and appeared to order another round of drinks.

Waiting at the bar, I could feel my brain ticking out an analysis of why I couldn't have fun. Perhaps the craziness of the club transported me back in time. As a teenager, I felt powerless to break out of my persona, incapable of acting outside my friends' or my family's or even Adam's expectations. Although all that stuff happened nearly fifteen years ago, it didn't seem like that long ago. It *felt* close. Or, maybe I had a hard time dealing with anxiety about the bar exam. The more I thought about it, the more I was sure I wouldn't see my name on the list.

Whatever the reason, I hated that it kept me from enjoying the moment. Because the moment would soon pass.

SHORTLY AFTER BEGINNING EIGHTH GRADE (THE SECOND OF TWO years in junior high), I made three new friends. Mike, Jim, and Pat.

I knew Mike the longest because his family went to my dad's church and we'd been involved in the same youth group for a couple years. He was a hyperactive kid, always looking for a good time even if it landed him in trouble. Although he played football, he never fit in with the jocks, probably because he was too much of a rebel. But I saw Mike as a funny, good-hearted guy.

Jim was the new kid, having moved to town the year before. While at school he acted like an introvert, outside those oppressive walls he exploded from his shell. He prided himself as a hacker. Whether installing viruses on school computers or stealing user passwords on AOL, he constantly invented ways to get us into trouble.

Pat acted as the leader of the group, perhaps because he had the most social standing among us. Tall, good-looking, and smart, everyone knew and liked him, especially girls. But he also carried an undercurrent of restlessness that seemed to come from a strained relationship with his highbrowed parents. You never knew what to expect from Pat—one day he'd be your best friend, the next day he wouldn't talk to you. I felt special the days he acted like my friend.

And then there was me. Principled yet doubtful. Outgoing yet pensive. Popular yet an outsider. Happy yet restless. Liked yet lonely.

The four of us often hung out after school and on weekends. Like my old friends, Mike, Jim, and Pat also drank and smoked. Unlike my old friends, though, they respected my decision not to partake. I never understood why it didn't bother them like it bothered Nicolas and those guys. Perhaps because like me, they didn't fit comfortably into any other social group and we were drawn together by a common sense of otherness.

I certainly knew I was different. I owned it too, carrying my straight-laced image like a badge of honor. But deep down I felt conflicted. Although I knew who I was supposed to be, I resented that my identity flowed from a refusal to bow to peer pressure. It pigeonholed me into a narrow range of behavior, and complying with everyone's expectations became a burden. If I gave in once, I abandoned my identity.

Pretty soon, I was saw every decision as a fork in the road. The summer after eighth grade, for instance, the four of us regularly slept over at Jim's house and snuck out at night. We would discreetly make our way through the neighborhood to a field behind my first elementary school. Under the cover of darkness, my friends would pop open a soda can, pour the drink onto the grass, poke a couple holes into its aluminum side, and use it as a makeshift pipe to smoke weed. I always stood a few feet back, watching as they got high.

Except one night.

Standing beside my friends in the middle of the field, crickets chirping in the distance, stars poured across the evening sky, I stepped forward and reached for the pipe. I was tired of feeling left out and different. I just wanted to belong.

But then I hesitated—and a thousand questions raced through my mind. How would this affect the rest of my life? Would I become like everyone else? What would people at school think—that I'd lost my religion? How would my parents react? Would the disappointment crush them? How would Adam respond? Would he ever speak to me again? What would become of my faith? Would it mean anything anymore? Would all my convictions suddenly disappear?

That night, I wanted so badly to step from one life, into another. But I couldn't. I didn't know how to be anyone other than me—and Paul Perkins *did not* smoke pot.

So I lowered my hand, stepped back, and continued watching.

After several hours of drinking and dancing, Eric signaled he wasn't feeling well. The four of us funneled out of the club, past the women hunting for prey, down the wooden stairway, and onto the dark streets of Kuta.

At the guesthouse, we stopped in front of my patio.

"Well, mate," Tom said, extending his hand. "It's been a real pleasure getting to know you."

I shook his hand, then pulled him in for a hug. "You too, Tom. Good luck with the surf school in Australia."

"Yeah, mate. You're a good man. Don't forget it."

Eric rested his arm on my shoulder. "I'm not sure how you made it out of Bali without getting trashed." His speech slurred and dark glasses covered his eyes. "But whatever. Go sue some people for us."

I laughed and, reaching my arm around Eric's shoulder, squeezed back. I glanced to my right and saw Brittany slowly shaking her head. Her eyes carried a heaviness, and it bothered me knowing I'd let her down. She pointed a finger at me and tightened her lips. I let go of Eric and stepped toward her.

"You know," she said, wrapping an arm around my shoulder and speaking quietly, "you really need to let go."

"I know. I'm just not much of a drinker, and the bar exam—"

"Stop." She dropped her arm and faced me. "No one asked you to get drunk. We just wanted to have fun. And you need to stop worrying about that damn test. You passed. And even if you fail, so what? Life goes on."

I looked down and sighed.

"But just for the record...." She looked away and swallowed hard. "You're a really sweet guy. And I'll miss you."

I reached toward Brittany and pulled her into my arms. "You're right." I breathed in slow and exhaled. "I'll miss you too."

By the time Brittany stepped back, we were alone. She smiled softly and we stood there looking at each other for a few seconds. Then she walked away and into her room.

As I stood alone in the garden, underneath the evening sky, I thought about how for years I struggled with two enormous choices. Right or wrong. Good or bad. Black or white. I viewed every decision through this lens. I thought it impossible to drink without getting drunk, or dance without partying, or date without having sex. I had no understanding of moderation. No concept of gradation. No sense of balance. My life was, for better or worse, all or nothing. So I never drank or danced or dated, because with a single misstep, I would no longer be myself—the "good Christian kid."

That's not how life works, though. Those are never the only two options. To think they were was both naive and wrong. Life is more complicated. The answers aren't always obvious. The right decision isn't always clear. And sometimes stepping outside the lines isn't so bad—maybe in the long run an occasional mistake is even good.

Perhaps as a teenager I clung to this false paradigm out of necessity, as a way to survive in a slippery-slope world where my identity felt constantly under attack. And the truth is, viewing life as two-toned shielded me from a lot of bad decisions. I never smoked pot or got drunk or slept around, which was certainly for the best.

Yet my unbending, stubborn perspective stunted my development, handicapping me relationally and emotionally. It also alienated me from my peers, leaving me susceptible to loneliness and isolation, a bad recipe for someone desperate for acceptance. Even my friendships with Mike, Jim, and Pat grew distant as our interests diverged.

So while this legalistic paradigm once served a limited purpose, as an adult it didn't make sense. I no longer needed a guardrail to keep me from slipping off the edge. I now had the mental and emotional maturity to see the grays. In fact, while living in DC I had already started living in the grays—dating and drinking and occasionally dancing—all without violating my sense of morality.

For some reason, though, I still lugged around my old identity, occasionally throwing it around my shoulders like a comfort blanket. Sometimes I not only acted like my teenage self, but I felt like him. And I didn't want to act or feel like someone who kept me from living so much life—friendships and love, mistakes and pain, happiness and joy.

It was time to let go of my past.

FOUR HOURS LATER MY ALARM WENT OFF. I STUMBLED OUT OF BED and shuffled across the street to an internet café. Sitting in front of a computer, I accessed the Oregon Bar website. The exam results hadn't posted yet, so I leaned back and anxiously watched the clock on the wall, tracking the second hand as it rotated, slowly nudging the hour hand toward a giant four.

If I saw my name on the list it meant I passed. If I didn't see my name, I failed. Pass or fail—two words that meant the difference between joy and pain, relief and disappointment, freedom and misery, life and death.

Then I recalled what Brittany had said about letting go. And in the back of my mind, I wondered if I also needed to let go of my future. What if, instead of worrying so much about what will happen next week, or next month, or next year, I focused on enjoying *this* moment—wherever I am, whatever I'm doing— and trusted God with my future? Because the truth is, whatever happened, pass or fail, I would be alright. Like Brittany said, life would go on.

There were more than two possibilities—there always have been. One failure wouldn't ruin this trip, and one mistake wouldn't ruin my life.

At four o'clock, I refreshed the website and clicked on the newly-appeared link for the bar exam results. As my hand shook with fear, I scrolled down to the letter P and scanned for my name. But I didn't see it. And my heart sank.

Then I scrolled up and saw: Paul Perkins.

I passed.

PART TWO
THAILAND

6

MEMORIES WITH MY BROTHER

I traveled to Thailand to visit my older brother, David. But as I sat on the twin-engine propeller plane, descending through the night sky toward city lights in the distance, I wondered if I was making a mistake.

For as long as I could remember, my brother and I had a strained relationship. As kids, he and our oldest brother, Ryan, both treated me badly. David, though, treated me the worst. Attempts to defend myself only made life harder. And because my parents couldn't moderate every dispute, I ended up learning to keep quiet and endure.

Still, I wanted my brothers to like me. I wanted them to treat me kindly and accept me. Sometimes that happened, but it never lasted long. In an instant they could turn. And that took its toll, leaving me with the helpless sense I couldn't protect myself. No one would keep me safe—not my parents, not my brothers, not even myself.

Looking back, I don't think I suffered any worse than a lot of kids with older brothers. Other than occasional punches to the arm, my brothers never physically harmed me. But I also have to remind myself that personal experience is subjective. What I went through, while perhaps not objectively terrible, felt like it at the time. That's what matters because it's what I lived.

That's why, sitting on an airplane approaching the island of Phuket, I began regretting my decision to visit David. I didn't want to be reminded of our past. I wanted to move on, and to me that meant continuing to keep my distance.

The plane landed with a thud and braked hard. I rubbed my eyes, dry from wearing contact lenses all day, and looked out the window into the evening darkness. Scattered lights on distant hills revealed silhouettes of palm trees.

After the seatbelt light turned off, I followed the other passengers out of the plane, across the tarmac, and into the airport. The terminal overflowed with families celebrating long-awaited reunions and tourists chatting among themselves. Hotel drivers stood against a wall, their faces tired, holding sheets of paper labeled with western names.

I zigzagged through the crowd in search of the exit. Once outside, buses, vans, cabs, and motor rickshaws trickled by, slowing to a near-standstill as they passed. Drivers, trying to establish eye contact, stalked me as if prey. Keeping my head down, I spotted a man on a motorcycle and, with a lift of my chin, caught his attention. He gassed the bike, squeezed between two buses, and appeared at my side.

"Where you go?" the driver asked. With saggy eyes and worn skin, he looked as though he'd earned each of his years alive. He wore faded khakis and a dark t-shirt that hung loosely over his body. His face, clean-shaven and plump, looked trustworthy.

"To Chalong," I said, tightening the straps around my backpack.

"Okay. I take you." He waved his palm toward the back of his motorcycle.

I stepped back. "Hold on. I should probably call my brother first to find out where he wants to meet."

The driver shook his head and frowned. "You have phone number?"

"Yeah." I pulled a scrap of paper out of my pocket, unfolded it, and showed it to him.

The driver lowered his eyes and examined my scribbles. "Okay, let's go." He nodded his head toward the back of the bike. "I call on way." He took the scrap out of my hand, then removed a cell phone from a pocket inside his jacket and held it up for me to see. "First let's get out of this mess."

I looked through the glass doors and into the airport. A small crowd stood in front of a luggage carousel carrying multicolored backpacks and battered suitcases. Those who found their bags were beginning to funnel into the pickup area, causing a stop-and-go bottleneck of vehicles. A cocktail of diesel and natural-gas exhaust saturated the air and a choir of multi-pitched horns pierced my ears. I looked back at the driver and noticed him eyeing another passenger.

"Fine," I said. Then I climbed onto the rear of the motor-cycle and, before I could secure my hands around the back rest, the bike jolted forward, exhaling a deep growl. I grabbed the driver's shoulders and held tight.

The bike slipped between vehicles, its horn tweeting rhythmically. We quickly reached an opening in the road and headed away from the airport—fast. I carefully readjusted, letting go of the driver and scooting to the back of the pillion. Then I clinched my right hand around the back rest and my left hand onto the edge of the leather seat.

Once stable, I looked at the evening sky. A soup of stars lit up the darkness. The moon, a glowing sliver, hung above the horizon, casting a light glow on the black concrete racing below my feet like a river of oil.

At an intersection the bike stopped. A two-lane highway ran perpendicular in front of us. The driver's head panned from one side to the other as he scanned for oncoming traffic. A green sign listed half a dozen cities and their distances.

"Thirty-five kilometers?" I asked, my voice drowned out by the rumble of a passing motorcycle.

Once it disappeared, the motor a fading hum, the driver responded. "Yes."

The bike accelerated into the intersection and swerved into an empty lane. Cruising at 80 kph, he reached into his jacket and pulled out the cell phone he had displayed earlier. With the other hand, he unfolded the scrap of paper with my brother's number and, pausing every few seconds to check the road, pecked each number into the phone with his index finger. He placed the phone between his shoulder and ear, and returned both hands to the handlebars.

"Hello. I am taxi driver and I have your brother. We are heading south toward Chalong."

Ten seconds passed before he spoke again. "Okay," he said, pausing briefly. "Yes, about fifteen minutes." The driver returned the phone to his jacket and held the scrap behind his shoulder.

I grabbed the paper and placed it inside my pants pocket. "Everything alright?"

He nodded. "Yes. We meet your brother at pier."

I eased my grip on the bike, reclined against the backrest, and watched the lone headlight pierce the darkness, exposing a narrow road and edges of a vegetation-covered landscape. The wind rushed around my face, colliding with the engine hum and an army of cicadas singing their evening song.

I closed my eyes and took a deep breath.

I WAS TEN YEARS OLD, SITTING IN THE BACKSEAT OF MY FAMILY'S DARK blue Oldsmobile 88. Ryan drove and David sat beside him in the passenger's seat. It was Sunday morning and we were on our way to church, cruising down Stafford Road, a steep, narrow two-lane road with four tight curves along the mile-long descent. It was a notoriously dangerous road, one most people drove slowly—well below the 35 mph speed limit. But not my brothers. And on that particular Sunday, the car raced down the hill, hurling past cars driving a quarter of our speed. Too Short blasted from treble-heavy speakers and my brothers talked about a party David went to the night before.

I leaned to my left and glanced at the speedometer between my brothers. We were going 50 mph. I watched the needle climb, then looked away. Shutting my eyes and tightening my jaw, I began praying. I'd heard stories during school assemblies about accidents that destroyed lives and ruined families. Some occurred on that very street. Earlier that summer, the police left a wrecked car on the side of the road for an entire week—a visual reminder that danger lurked around every corner.

Halfway down the hill, we careened into the second curve, slipping on a patch of gravel. Fear squeezed my stomach and my mind blanked. Ryan quickly corrected the steering and stomped on the accelerator. My brothers' conversation continued uninterrupted, as though we hadn't almost slid off the road into a forest of evergreen trees below.

"Hey," I said, my voice struggling to rise above the music. "Could you please slow down?"

My brothers stopped talking. Hollow beats and profanity-laced rhymes filled the car. David turned around in his seat and stared at me. He looked angry. Then, with a few choice words, he made me regret speaking up.

SITTING ON THE BACK OF THE MOTORCYCLE, I NOTICED MY JAW GROWing sore from clenching my teeth. The taxi driver and I were traveling along a wide road with vehicles parked on both sides. A car or motorbike occasionally passed in the opposite direction. Darkened storefronts aged by weather occupied the left side of the road and palm trees lined the right. Beyond the trees stretched the Andaman Sea—an eternity of darkness at this hour. Across its pitch-black surface reflected a pale imitation of the Milky Way.

Slowing the motorcycle, the driver took a sharp turn, then stopped in the middle of an empty parking lot.

He got off the bike and said, "We meet your brother here." Then he pulled a pack of cigarettes from his shirt pocket, shook out a smoke, raised it to his lips, and kissed the tip with a match. He inhaled deeply, the ash growing a furious red. Then he exhaled, white puffs drifting out of his mouth, and a moment later, disappearing into the air. He tossed the match onto the pavement and faced the sea.

"Sounds good," I said as I stepped onto the ground. I sat my backpack down and pulled my wallet from my back pocket. After handing the driver a few paper bills, I made my way across the parking lot. With every step, the ocean waves grew louder until they sounded all around me.

At the edge of a sidewalk, I stared into the darkness, listening to the ocean's thrashing. Then I noticed a long pier extending into the sea. Like discovering a constellation among the jumbled mess of stars, I couldn't believe I hadn't noticed it when we arrived. Somehow I had overlooked the obvious.

From behind, a succession of horns pierced the ocean's roar. I turned and saw a single headlight bouncing up and down. It turned from the road and into the parking lot, then continued toward me, growing by the second. It raced past the taxi driver as he sucked on a half-finished cigarette. Then it stopped in front of me.

It was David sitting on an old black motorcycle. A white, full-faced helmet with a dark visor covered his head, and he wore gray jeans and a black t-shirt. He appeared healthier than last time I saw him. Then he removed his helmet. Black stitches lined his forehead above his right eye, which was bruised purple.

"Whoa," I said. "What happened to your face?"

"The other night I was driving home from the pharmacy," he said with a grin, "and decided to take a nap."

"Bad time for a nap, I guess."

He laughed, then slid off his bike and hugged me. "Welcome to Thailand, little bro."

I hugged back and said, "Thanks."

"How was your flight?"

"Alright. Let me grab my backpack then we can take off. Maybe we can get something to eat?"

"Cool."

I jogged across the parking lot and found the driver sitting on his idling motorcycle. His cigarette, a stub tipped with grey ash, was perched in the corner of his mouth between his lips.

"Okay, my friend," he said. "Good luck."

I shook his hand. "Thanks for the ride."

After exchanging nods, the driver tossed the cigarette butt onto the pavement, then accelerated out of the parking lot.

"You ready?" David shouted, driving his bike toward me. "Put this on." He tossed his helmet into the air.

I caught it and placed it over my head. "Don't you need it?"

He inched the bike forward, dragging his shoes against the pavement. "It's the only one I've got and you've more to protect up there than me."

I laughed. "I'm not so sure. But thanks."

I slipped my arms between my backpack straps, stepped over the seat, and sat behind David. He gassed the bike and we sped across the parking lot and onto the road. Following the shoreline, we gradually gained speed. I tightened my grip around the frame and watched the sea, its waves battering the shoreline.

ONE SATURDAY IN EIGHTH GRADE, I STAYED UP LATE WATCHING TV with David and his friend, Daniel, when they decided to go to Taco Bell. I asked to come along, and neither of them seemed to care. So the three of us loaded into Daniel's grey 1966 Mercedes, a beat-up classic sporting a column-mounted shifter and a high-beam floorboard clicker.

After driving across town and eating, we headed back home.

"Those tacos were good," David said, "but I'm still hungry."

"Yeah," Daniel said. "Whaddya got in mind?"

"Ice cream, beer, and girls."

Daniel laughed. "I was thinking the same thing."

"Great," David said. "We'll swing by Baskin Robbins then hit up Laura's party."

I looked at my watch—it was a quarter till midnight. "Can you just drop me off at home?"

My brother sighed. "Paul, you're always such a downer. Why'd you wanna tag along anyway?"

I lowered my face into my hands. Rubbing my eyes, a knot formed in my throat and I swallowed hard. When I looked up, I caught my brother's reflection in the rearview mirror. He looked hard. Detached. "And why do you wanna get drunk?"

David laughed. And then he tore into me.

A GUST OF WIND BLEW AGAINST ME, CLEARING THE MOISTURE FROM my helmet. Stopped at a red light on a busy four-lane highway, we waited for the light to turn green. Half-completed construction projects lined the left side of the road. On the right, I spotted a convenience store with a food cart beside it. A few people stood in front of the cart and someone sat at a picnic table.

"Does that work?" David asked, pointing his elbow at the food cart.

"Yeah."

The light turned green and we sped through the intersection. David flicked on the right turn signal and slowed to a stop, waiting for a clearing in the traffic. The bike struggled to remain upright as it hugged the yellow divider-line. Vehicles raced by in opposite directions, leaving a wake of rushing wind. At a small break in the traffic, David accelerated the bike across the yellow line, and we flew through two lanes and into a dirt parking lot, then stopped with a halt. A cloud of dust enveloped us and then dispersed into the air.

I quickly stepped off the bike, anxious to plant my feet on the earth. Then I removed the helmet and followed David to the food cart. Two people stood in front of us, and behind the cart, a woman scooped soup out of a large metal pot and poured it into a ceramic bowl. A handwritten sign listed three items. Although I couldn't read Thai, the choices were obvious: soup, bottled water, and Coke.

When we reached the counter, David spoke. "Two soups," he said, miming a bowl, "a Coke," he continued, pointing at the glass bottles behind the woman, "and—" he turned toward me, "water or Coke?"

"Water," I responded, pointing at a plastic bottle.

The woman smiled shyly and turned to gather our meal. My brother removed 30 baht from his pocket and placed it on the counter.

"Thanks," I said, handing him three coins. "I only have five baht. I'll pay you the rest later."

He took the change and dropped it into his jeans pocket. "No worries."

The woman turned around and set two bowls, a water bottle, and a glass bottle of Coke on the counter. Steam rose from the soup and condensation coated the bottles. We each took our food, then headed to the white picnic table. I sat across from David, facing the four-lane highway, and watched as he raised the wide spoon to his mouth and lowered it into the bowl.

ONE EVENING WHEN I WAS ELEVEN, I STEPPED INTO OUR HOME AND saw a group of adults in the living room. My parents sat on a couch and everyone else faced them, sitting in chairs. I recognized some of the adults as parents of David's friends. For some reason, I sensed something bad had happened to him, and that worried me.

I stood with the front door open, cold air slipping inside, and studied their faces. The women looked concerned and some held tissues. One man was the dad of David's best friend. He rested his head against his hand and tightly clinched his other hand into a fist. My dad sat forward, resting his elbows on his knees. Speaking in his preaching voice, he gestured fluidly with his hands. When he glanced at me, I shut the door and ran upstairs, into my room.

Laying on my bed, I tried to interpret the tone of muffled voices carrying through the walls. But I couldn't make out the words. So I just lay there, my fear growing by the minute. Once everything quieted down, I found my mom in the kitchen. Her eyes looked puffy.

I sat on the hardwood floor next to our cocker spaniel and rubbed his head. "What happened?" I asked.

My mom walked over to me and bent down. Then she took a deep breath. "Your dad and I found out something about your brother."

"What?"

"He's—" my mom paused, "been living a secret life."

I shook my head. "What do you mean?"

She looked away and then back at me. "For the past couple years, he's been getting drunk with his friends."

I looked at my mom confused. Her words didn't make sense. To my young mind, getting drunk was something only bad people did. I couldn't understand why David would do that. He had everything going for him—he was funny and popular and athletic and artistic. Why would he risk it all? Why would he choose to hurt himself?

Despite all the teasing and ridicule, I still looked up to him and even admired him. When he was nice, he was one of my favorite people. Following him in school by three years, I always lived in his shadow, never quite as cool or funny or popular as him—but that didn't bother me. I was proud he was my brother, honored I could claim him as my own.

But David getting drunk, I couldn't understand it. It didn't add up.

SLICES OF GREEN ONION STUCK TO THE BOTTOM OF THE EMPTY BOWL. I set the spoon down and watched David hold the Coke to his mouth and swallow. The liquid quickly drained from the bottle, and he set it on the table. Beads of dew dribbled down the glass, collecting at the ribbed bottom and pooling on the table.

He stood from the chair and reached for my bowl. "You finished?"

"Yeah," I said, stretching my arms behind my back, then yawning.

He picked up both bowls, placed the empty bottles inside of them, and walked to the food cart. After leaving the dishes on the counter, he reached inside his pocket and fished out the coins I gave him. Then he set them on the counter by the cash register.

"Khob khun krab," he said.

The woman smiled and bowed her head.

"You ready?" he asked, signaling for me to follow him.

"Yeah." I stood from the chair, slid it under the table, and jogged past him to the motorcycle. "I heard you're not supposed to leave tips in Thailand," I said, stepping over the bike and sitting on the black leather seat.

He sat in front of me and started the engine. "What do you mean?"

I placed the helmet over my head and flipped up the visor. "Someone in Bali told me Thais don't like tips because, as Buddhists, karmic equilibrium will require them to provide charity to others."

David laughed. "That might be true. But I bet they secretly like it."

A trail of dust followed us across the parking lot as we merged onto the highway.

STANDING IN FRONT OF A PIANO KEYBOARD IN MY SIXTH GRADE MUSIC class, I felt mischievous. Three rows of students stood in front of me, each with their own keyboard. The teacher, Ms. Ball, sat behind an upright cherry wood piano at the front of the classroom. She'd spent the entire class teaching us Beethoven's "Ode to Joy."

My friend, Nicolas, stood beside me, pecking his keyboard in sync with everyone else.

"Check this out," I whispered, raising my eyebrows playfully.

Nicolas glanced at me, then back at his keyboard, his fingers continuing to rise and fall across the black and white keys. When the song reached a pause, I leaned across his keyboard and pressed the green "Demo" button. A succession of bongo drums blasted from his speakers, followed by a synthesizer-heavy dance groove designed to showcase the keyboard's instruments.

Everyone stopped, turned around, and looked at Nicolas. His jaw dropped and he took a step away from the keyboard.

"Paul," he yelled. Then he began shifting his shoulders to the beat of the song.

I tossed my hands over my mouth and started giggling. A small group of students turned back around and picked up where they left off, "Ode to Joy" ringing out against the laughter and catchy beat. A handful of our friends joined the chaos, raising their hands into the air and dancing. The rest of the class watched in amusement as Ms. Ball stood from her piano bench and raced through the rows of students to the back of the classroom.

Nicolas slammed his hand across the keyboard, hitting a few buttons, one of which ended the song.

Ms. Ball stopped in front of me, her face cold and rigid. "See me after class."

Once class ended and the room emptied, I shut the door. With my hands jammed into my jeans pockets, I tiptoed to the front of the room and stopped beside Ms. Ball's piano. While I stared at the light blue, tightly wound carpet, Ms. Ball watched me. Then she walked past me. I followed close behind, grazing the soles of my shoes against the carpet, creating a soft whooshing sound. At the door, she stopped, turned around, and looked down at me.

"Your brother was in my class three years ago," she said, enunciating each word carefully.

I looked away from the floor and up at Ms. Ball. She squinted her icy blue eyes and pressed her thin pale lips together. Her long, narrow nose pointed straight at me.

"And what you did," she continued, slowly shaking her head, "I would've expected from him." She paused and looked into my eyes. "But not from you."

Her words knocked me dizzy. My eyes dropped to the floor and I struggled to swallow the rock lodged in my throat. But I couldn't. It felt like she poked a finger into a gaping chest wound. I blinked a couple times and my chin quivered.

"I'm sorry," I said quietly.

WITHOUT SLOWING, THE MOTORCYCLE JERKED ACROSS TWO EMPTY lanes and onto a narrow road winding through a neighborhood. I grabbed David's shoulder to keep from sliding off the seat. We drove fast, passing small houses with yards of patchy grass and stringy bushes. After a few blocks, we began going up a hill, quickly gaining elevation.

"I'm staying at the top of the hill," he said, leaning back for me to hear. Then he squeezed the accelerator. The higher we climbed, the faster we moved. Near the top, a dog bolted from a garage and began chasing us. David laid on the horn and accelerated even faster.

In front of a whitewashed condominium, he pulled into a driveway and stopped. I stepped off the bike, placed the helmet on the seat, and walked to a railing overlooking the city. Lights flickered across the valley to the Andaman Sea and up a mountain to the east.

"You ready?" he asked, placing his hand on my shoulder as he walked by me.

Ignoring his question, I continued staring at the distant lights.

THE CALL CAME FOUR DAYS AFTER CHRISTMAS, DURING MY SOPHO-more year of college. My whole family was together, celebrating the holiday. The woman on the phone said she was from the hospital where my dad's father, Lynn, had been diagnosed with pneumonia earlier in the day. My dad had been with him and assured us it didn't seem serious. He certainly didn't look sick when we piled into his apartment two days earlier and showered him with presents. According to the nurse on the phone, though, he was failing. So we quickly piled into two cars and headed to the hospital.

Lynn, whom we called Gramps, lived with us from the time I was in fifth grade until the summer after I graduated from high school. He was a tough guy—a man's man. But when he moved in with us, he was a defeated man. He had just suffered a second stroke and his wife of fifty-five years no longer wanted him around. None of his three daughters could take him, either, so my dad eagerly assumed the responsibility. He looked forward to starting fresh with his father and forming a close relationship—unlike what he had growing up.

But it never quite worked out like that. Gramps mostly stayed in his bedroom and watched television, occasionally venturing out to give my dad a hard time or talk football.

Over the years, Gramps' spirit lifted and he began spending more time with our family. He celebrated holidays and birthdays with us, and sometimes dressed up to watch my dad preach on Sunday mornings. Occasionally I walked with him around the neighborhood and listened to him tell stories about serving in the military during World War II and driving across Texas selling insurance. David liked taking Gramps to his favorite restaurant, Denny's, and eating Klondike bars together.

For some reason, Gramps bonded best with David. Perhaps he saw part of himself in him—the wild spirit, the risk-taker, the rebel. Whatever it was, they shared a deep connection, a common understanding unlike with any of us, even my dad.

At the hospital, we rushed through empty hallways until we found the right unit. My dad pushed open the double doors and everyone followed close behind. I'll never forget what I heard next.

A deep, pained groan.

We rushed into Gramps' room and circled his bed. Tubes ran from his nose, down his ashen arms, into a machine. He inhaled and exhaled as though his lungs couldn't hold air. A blue gown loosely draped his skeletal frame. And then there were his blue, blue eyes—betraying every ounce of fear within.

Between gasps, he whispered, "I'm suffocating."

My dad bent beside Gramps and grasped his still-muscular forearm. "We're here for you, dad," he said softly. "Your family is here for you."

My mom stood behind my dad, and my two brothers stood beside me at the end of the bed. I made eye contact with Ryan and then looked at David. Tears pooled in his eyes.

After a while, my dad told us he'd stay with Gramps through the night, but the rest of us could go home. He suggested we each say something before leaving. My mom spoke first, then Ryan. When it was David's turn, he stepped to the side of the bed, lowered to his knees, and took Gramps' hand. Then he looked into his eyes.

"I love you," he said, his voice quivering. "And I'll miss you so much."

David stood and returned to the edge of the bed. As I passed by him, he gently placed his hand on my shoulder.

Standing before Gramps, I tried to speak, but nothing came out. All I could think about was the overwhelming sadness in the room—the fear in Gramps' eyes, the end of a tragic life, the buried pain between my dad and his father, the shock on everyone's face. I bent down, cupped my hand over Gramps' ear, and whispered, "I love you."

A couple hours later, I left the hospital with my mom and Ryan. My dad and David stayed with Gramps through the night.

And they were by his side, with their hands resting on his chest, when he breathed his final breath.

WHEN I HEARD THE FRONT DOOR OPEN, I PULLED MYSELF AWAY FROM the railing.

"Nice view," I said, stepping into the condo after David.

"Not bad, eh? I'm keeping an eye on my friend's place till she returns from a visa run."

"Good deal."

He led me down a hallway with Asian art decorating the walls, through a living room with a fluffy white couch, and into a small bedroom. There was a queen-size bed in the corner and a grey sleeping bag on the floor. Across the room, a floor-to-ceiling window opened onto the city and the sea beyond. I set my backpack down and lay on the sleeping bag, resting my head on a pillow.

"Tired?" David asked, looking down at me.

"Yeah," I said, struggling to suppress a yawn. "I've been traveling all day."

"I'll be right back."

David walked out of the room, and a moment later, I heard a door shut and a faucet turn on—and I couldn't help wondering if he was washing his face or getting high.

DAYS AFTER I RETURNED TO OREGON AND MOVED INTO MY PARENTS' guestroom, I got a call from David. It'd been a while, and he wanted to hang out. We decided to go Christmas shopping on

Hawthorne Boulevard, an artsy district in Portland with eclectic shops and used clothing stores.

I drove into Portland and met him in front of a coffee shop. He wore a navy blue peacoat and held a Gatorade in one hand and a cigarette in the other. As I followed him from store to store, we made small talk, but I had a hard time engaging. My mind was elsewhere, focused on the task before me—studying for the bar exam. Spending an afternoon with David seemed a distraction.

Then he pulled a wallet from his pocket to buy something, and I saw his hand shaking. He was high, probably on heroin. Immediately I told him I had to go. He asked why, and I made up an excuse. Then I left.

Other than some passing interactions over the next few weeks, that was one of the last times I'd seen him.

I MUST HAVE FALLEN ASLEEP, BECAUSE I DIDN'T NOTICE DAVID RETURN and get into his bed.

"The bathroom's around the corner," he said.

I found my toiletry bag in my backpack and headed to the bathroom. After removing my contacts, brushing my teeth, and washing my face, I returned to the bedroom. The lights were off, so I quietly slipped into the sleeping bag on the floor. Then I laid my head on a pillow and turned toward the window. City lights still sparkled in the distance. The Andaman Sea, with its ink-black, almost motionless ripples slowly shifting, still reflected a distorted mirror image of the scattered stars. The cicadas still sang their evening song.

As my eyes shut, I thought about all the pain separating me from David. All the times he picked on me; all the times he made fun of me; all the times I felt helpless before him. The memories weighed heavy on me, and I nearly shifted my mind to more pleasant thoughts—like my reunion with Alissa in India.

But then I pushed myself to consider other memories with my brother. The love he showed Gramps throughout the final years of his life and on his deathbed. The fear I felt when I learned he started drinking. The sadness I felt when my music teacher disrespected him. The times we had fun together growing up, biking around the neighborhood and playing at the beach and watching movies. The occasional generosity he showed me as a child—sharing candy and including me in sleepovers with his friends. The fact that, because he was my brother, I knew nobody would mess with me when I walked into high school as a freshman.

Then I thought about all the times he reached out to me over the years; all the times he treated me with respect as adults; all the times he made an effort to connect with me. I thought about the times he checked himself into rehab, and the courage it took to continue fighting a years-long battle with addiction and mental illness. I thought about the time his best friend committed suicide, and the crushing pain and regret he must have suffered dealing with that tragedy. I thought about the time he developed a serious staph infection, and the fear of knowing I might lose my brother. I thought about the risk he took leaving Oregon and moving to Thailand—escaping his universe and desperately trying to rescue his life. And I wondered if maybe I had misjudged him.

It had been easy to cast him as the bad guy—to hold on to all the pain and anger and bitterness leftover from my childhood. But maybe he deserved more grace, because maybe he was more complicated. Not filled with hate, but full of hurt. Perhaps the reasons he lashed out at me had more to do with his own pain than anything else. Maybe I wasn't the only victim. Maybe he was a victim too.

As I neared sleep, I heard David's voice. "Goodnight."

I opened my eyes. "Goodnight."

After a few seconds he said, "I'm glad you're here, little bro."

I turned and looked up toward his bed. The stars and city lights shone through the window casting just enough light to see his silhouette. "So am I." I paused briefly. "So am I."

7

ALONE IN PARADISE

The aging road hugged the rocky shoreline of the Andaman Sea. Turquoise water stretched to the horizon, blending sea with sky. Squinting, a narrow white line emerged in the distance, dividing the ocean from the noontime sky. I shifted my eyes back to the weathered road.

"It's a bit further," David shouted over the sound of our engines.

He accelerated his motorcycle around a corner and I followed close behind on a red Vespa. As the road tapered, I struggled to keep the scooter from scraping against a rock wall on one side and tumbling off a 300-foot cliff on the other side. My eyes narrowed and my grip tightened as I rounded a sharp turn then climbed a hill into a shaded jungle. The light dimmed and the ocean vanished from view. The air, mercilessly hot a moment before, suddenly felt balmy and damp. A canopy of branches formed an umbrella high above and hanging vines swayed with the breeze.

Without slowing, David veered across the road and disappeared down a steep hill. I eased on the brakes to make sure vehicles weren't heading in the opposite direction, then crept across the road and down the hill onto a beat-up driveway. With large chunks of missing pavement and loose gravel eroding at the edges, it looked like a jackhammer had attacked it. I slowly snaked down the hill, jolting over every rock and divot.

At the bottom, I let the engine peter out next to David's bike. He stood at the edge of the gravel lot, staring into the distance. I walked toward him and stopped by his side. Then I looked around, taking in my surroundings.

A forest of trees crowded behind us, reaching hundreds of feet into the air, blocking sunlight. Steps away, shade gave way to white sand that wrapped around a crescent bay. Vertical cliffs closed off one end, and the other end opened to a stretch of beach extending half a mile down the shoreline, thick vegetation bordering its edges. Crystal blue water lapped against the spotless sand and two kids played on the shore, their parents lying on towels nearby. Hundreds of yards offshore, boulders jutted from the sea as though dropped by prehistoric giants. Dark lines streaked their sides and waves crashed against them. Near the end of the narrow stretch of beach, between the ocean and the forest, I spotted a row of cabins.

"What do you think?" David asked.

I glanced at him and could tell he relished introducing me to this place. His eyes were fixed on the horizon and he slowly nodded his head. "It's beautiful," I said, shifting my eyes to the ocean. "Are you sure you don't want to hang out here for a few nights?"

David took a step back. "No thanks, bro. I've got too much going on this week."

"That's cool." I paused, scratching the side of my head. "Well, thanks for bringing me out here."

"No worries."

David put his arms around me and squeezed tight, and I hugged back. I didn't want him to leave—but I knew he had to go. Not just for himself, but for me too.

Over the past month in Indonesia, I'd been surrounded by people. While it'd been fun, it hadn't provided much time to reflect. And I had a big decision ahead of me—my relationship with Alissa had grown increasingly serious since the beginning of my trip. We'd sent dozens of emails back and forth, pouring our hearts out and letting each other into our lives. I wondered if we were falling in love. When we met in India in two months, I suspected we would talk about our future together, perhaps even the prospect of marriage.

"Have a good time," David said. Then he turned around and headed toward his motorcycle. Halfway there, he looked back and shouted, "Call if you wanna grab dinner or something. I'm only twenty minutes away."

"Cool."

As I watched David start his bike and zigzag up the steep driveway, I felt an emptiness crack open. I didn't do well in isolation. It's part of the reason I opted to live with roommates—that, and the cost-savings. Loneliness had a way of pulling me down. The best way to escape it, I had learned, was with action.

So I turned around and took a step toward the ocean. Inches away, dirt transitioned into sand and shade gave way to light. A breeze brushed against my face and salty air filled my lungs. My eyes drifted to the blur on the horizon and I listened to each successive wave surging onto the shore and, just as quickly, rushing back into the ocean.

At the far end of the gravel lot, I noticed a dark wood cabin with a tin roof and a large open window on one side. I walked over to it and saw a woman inside, flipping through a magazine. She had short grey hair and brown weathered skin. When she noticed me, she smiled softly.

"You lookin' for cabin?"

"I am," I said, leaning my arm on a shelf below the window. "For five nights, if possible."

She looked at me suspiciously. "You alone?"

I nodded.

"You're lucky," she said, raising her eyebrows. "We have one left."

"That's all I need."

We agreed to a price and she slid a binder in front of me. I opened to the last page and wrote my name, passport number, and country of origin. When I looked up, the woman dug a key out of her pocket and tossed it at me. I caught it, then placed cash on the shelf.

"Head that way," she said, pointing down the shoreline. "It's cabin seven."

I thanked the woman and followed a dirt trail toward the beach. Before stepping onto the sand I took off my flip-flops. Then I walked to the edge of the ocean and let a wave submerge my feet—like in Bali, the water was bathtub warm, and I couldn't wait to get in. I looked up at the sky, which was fading dark blue as the day progressed, and saw the sun at its apex.

Then I continued along the water's edge toward the row of cabins in the distance. The family I saw a while ago now ate lunch at a picnic table. After passing them, the two kids bolted by me with flailing arms, turned toward the ocean, and collided with a wave. As they ran out of the water, laughter exploded from their mouths. They plopped onto a patch of dry sand and began repairing a collapsed sandcastle.

"Hallo," the older kid said as I walked past them.

"Hi there," I said, eyeing their project. The damage looked irreparable and I doubted they had the time or patience to fix it. One of them would give up, then the other would follow. Pretty soon there would be no trace of it other than fading memories.

As I neared the cabins, I noticed a couple relaxing on the beach. They were around my age, maybe a few years older, and seemed oblivious to everything around them. The ocean muffled their voices, but occasionally I heard the girl laugh. Seeing them reminded me of Alissa, and I felt a pang of loneliness return. I quickly looked away and continued toward the cabins.

When I arrived at the first cabin, I couldn't believe what I saw. Constructed with wood logs and outfitted with panoramic windows, it looked like a masterpiece. I spotted a small "1" painted in white above the front door, and figured my cabin was the last of the remaining six.

I continued down the shore, gliding my feet above the sand and dipping my hand into water that reached me. To keep from feeling down, I reminded myself that the beauty of this place crushed everywhere else in comparison—better than rainy Portland and the concrete jungle of DC.

Eventually I reached the final cabin on the beach. Though the smallest of the lot and constructed with wood slats rather than logs or bricks, the setting was idyllic. Paradise. Easily the most stunning place of my trip thus far. I hoped to start feeling better once I got settled—not so scattered and restless.

I leapt up the stairs two at a time and slipped the key into a padlock on the front door. The lock clicked. After removing the padlock, I pushed open the door and walked inside. Although it wasn't the dirtiest place I'd stayed, it was the most meager. It looked the size of a walk-in closet with a tiny bathroom attached. A twin futon occupied three-quarters of the room, and I didn't see electrical outlets. The lack of standard comforts didn't bother me, though. What concerned me were the one-inch gaps in the wood-slate floors and light seeping through the edges of the shutter windows.

I didn't want anything disturbing my stay in paradise—and that meant no insects or rodents. As long as I kept the light off at night, I figured I'd be fine. Plus I already paid for the room and didn't want to go through the hassle of finding a nicer place. On my budget, that actually might not have been possible.

Near the edge of the futon, I set my backpack on the floor and unpacked all my belongings onto three wooden shelves built into the wall. On the top shelf, I left two sacks from a bakery David and I ate breakfast at earlier in the day. One held tomorrow's breakfast: a mango, lychee, and rambutan. The other contained the real treasure: a slice of coconut bread and a loaf of banana bread the size of a brick. The smell made my mouth salivate. But I didn't want to give in just yet.

After arranging my things, I sat on the futon and thought about writing in my journal. I'd been meaning to process my thoughts and emotions. It seemed like too much effort and con-templation, though, and I suspected it would only make matters worse. So I changed into shorts and a t-shirt, laced my shoes, and headed back outside.

Running, I quickly passed the now-deserted spot where I'd seen the young couple, the sandcastle breached by the ocean's tide, and the perfect family walking toward the magnificent cabin. At the dirt trail, I took a sharp turn and proceeded past the wood shack, continued through the gravel lot, and sprinted up the driveway. Then I stopped to catch my breath and stretch.

Once I felt loose, I began running toward a bright light in the distance—where the jungle ended and sunlight struck the pave-ment. A soft breeze nudged me forward and drops of dew sprin-kled from the vegetation above. It felt good to use my muscles again—refreshing. It energized me and I felt a tinge of optimism.

Then I left the jungle. With no clouds overhead, the sun scorched everything in sight. I started by running on the left side of the road, beside the rock wall, but I couldn't stand the heat's radiation. So I crossed the street and continued along the edge of the cliff—one wrong step from death.

Twenty minutes into the run, I felt a wave of nausea and slowed my pace. Then a breeze rolled in from the ocean, provid-ing precious seconds of relief. As the air grew stagnant again, the heat returned—and the back of my head began pounding. I slipped my shirt off and placed it inside my shorts, between the elastic band and my waist, then brushed a hand through my hair. I jogged up a few hills, rounded a bend, dodged a motorbike, and finally descended a hill into a small town.

I slowed to a walk, then made my way past several storefronts and a fruit juice stand. At the end of the block, I circled back and picked up a banana smoothie, then headed across the street to a lookout point.

Below, throngs of people were spread across a beach—some lying in the sun, others bobbing in the ocean. A group of teenagers bodysurfed waves as they rolled in, reminding me of surfing with Tom, Eric, and Brittany. It'd only been a couple days since leaving them in Bali, but it seemed a lifetime ago. Perhaps that's because I was two thousand miles away.

Then I noticed a couple walking along the shoreline, hand in hand, sharing what seemed to be a romantic moment. I wondered if it was the same couple I saw near my cabin. The guy had short dark hair and a lean physique, and the girl had blonde hair and a thin, hourglass figure. I watched as he whispered into her ear and she tossed her head back, presumably laughing. With his arm around her waist, he pulled her close and their bodies touched. Then they kissed.

I quickly turned and started running—up the hill, around the bend, down two shallow hills, and along a straightaway. Once I reached the shaded jungle, my run turned into a sprint. I booked it as fast as I could, against burning lungs and rubber legs, until I reached the top of the driveway. After resting a minute, I meandered back to the cabin.

I still didn't feel like journaling and I definitely didn't feel up to the task of praying—so I changed into a swimsuit, snatched my mask and snorkel, and headed back outside. A warm breeze blew from the ocean and the sun dropped toward the horizon. I waded into the water and continued out until my hips were submerged. Then I placed the mask over my face, slipped the snorkel into my mouth, and lunged forward.

Floating on my stomach with my face in the water, I swam to the middle of the bay and then back and forth, from one side to the other, exploring schools of exotic fish and coral life. Every so often, I held my breath and dove underwater. Kicking my feet, I swam as deep as possible, all the while taking in everything around me. Creatures with bulging eyes and smashed noses. Light shining both bright and dim. Muted yet elongated sounds. Even the sun had a way of shimmering through the water, activating sparkles previously asleep.

I had so much fun I lost track of time. When I peered above the water, the sun hung just above the ocean. One final time, I dove underwater. Around ten feet, I turned around to look up at the surface. As my body starved for air, I watched ripples of water dance with beams of sunlight—it was a beautiful few moments, quiet and peaceful, and I didn't want it to end.

After swimming to shore, I found a dry spot on the beach and sat down. Distant waves crashed against rock walls and water lapped against the shore. The sun bled into the ocean and the sky faded iris blue. With so much beauty in front of me, I expected to feel happier—more content and less empty. But I sensed something missing. The loneliness I felt earlier in the day hadn't gone away. It had only compounded.

Back at the cabin, I took a cold shower. Walking out of the bathroom, I glanced around my room. That's when I *knew* something was gone. My eyes shifted to the shelves—my camera, journal, and laptop were safe, and so were my clothes. Then I saw the pastry sack on the top shelf. Like a deflated balloon, it looked empty.

I rushed over to examine it and quickly identified a small hole in the corner with crumbs of banana bread littering the shelf. With an index finger, I lifted the opening and peeked inside. The coconut bread still smelled delicious, but an edge looked nibbled at—it was hard to tell. That wasn't the worst discovery, though. The loaf of banana bread had vanished.

Confused, I looked behind my items on the other two shelves. Neither turned up the missing banana bread. Then it dawned on me—someone or something stole it. I suspected it wasn't a person. That didn't make sense. The only possibility, then, was a rodent. And that creeped me out. It also frustrated me. I'd looked forward to enjoying that treat since I purchased it hours earlier. Now it was gone.

I returned to the bathroom and grabbed a hanger that served as a makeshift towel rack. On one end of the hanger I tied the fruit sack, and on the other end I tied the pastry sack. Then I hung the contraption from a nail protruding off the top shelf. What remained of my food was now safe and secure—feet above the floor and inches from the shelf.

After getting dressed, I headed back outside to the wood shack. A man now sat behind the desk with his feet propped on the guest registration binder. Deep wrinkles stretched across his forehead and his eyes looked tired.

"Can I make a call?" I asked, pointing to a phone on the desk.

He glanced at the phone and then at me. "Local?"

I nodded.

He picked up the phone and set it on the shelf below the window. I took the receiver and dialed David's number. After a few rings he answered.

"What's up?" he said.

"Not much. Just seeing if you want to grab dinner."

"I wish I could, bro. Let's chill in a few days, alright?"

"Sure. Maybe we can visit Patong one night."

"If you want," he said with a chuckle. "So how's paradise treatin' ya?"

"It's alright. I went for a jog along the ocean. Swam with some fish. Sat on the beach. Took a cold shower. Hid my food."

David laughed. "Sounds like fun."

"Yeah. I guess so."

"You guess?"

I paused. "Yeah. I guess."

"Well, try to enjoy dinner."

"Talk to you later."

I hung up the phone and found my motor scooter in the gravel lot. After carefully working my way up the driveway, I followed the coastline, shifting my eyes back and forth from the road to the sunset. Orange streaks flared across the sky and cirrus clouds radiated like searing coals as the final tip of the sun melted into the horizon. The ocean, now navy blue, dimly reflected the sky's brilliant colors.

The restaurant was a small dive serving cheap local dishes. Looking over the menu, I debated whether to branch out and try something new but instead ordered my favorite, Pad Thai. I savored the meal, then reclined in my seat and opened *Life of Pi*, a story about a kid stranded in the ocean on a boat with a tiger. I know everyone feels this way when reading a good book, but I really did identify with the kid. Not necessarily the tiger part, just about being alone in paradise.

I read a chapter, then dropped 40 baht on the table and stood to leave. The only other customers in the restaurant, a middle-aged couple sharing a beer, glanced at me as I walked past them. I sensed they felt bad for me, eating alone and all.

When I stepped outside, a full moon shined bright overhead. Even without streetlamps, it provided enough light to navigate the roads even without a headlight. I started the motor scooter and took off toward my cabin. Moonlight reflected off the ocean, displaying a single light in a sea of darkness. My eyes teared up from air rushing past my face. Gripping the rubber handlebars, my hands vibrated with the engine and felt every rise and drop of the road. I took slow, successive breaths, filling my lungs with moist ocean air. Peace, I sensed, approached.

After passing into the jungle, I crossed the street at the turn-off and cautiously proceeded down the driveway. Then I headed to the beach. I'd had a good day—running and snorkeling and watching the sunset and eating a delicious dinner. But I felt bad about not journaling or spending time in prayer. I really did want God's counsel in my relationship with Alissa. I suppose I was just afraid what he would say. My feelings for Alissa were stronger than ever, yet something held me back, keeping me from *fully* committing.

As I neared my cabin, I saw a faint light in the distance. At first I thought it was a campfire—maybe the young couple had returned to taunt me again. But then I realized it was too small to be a campfire. It looked more like a flashlight or...a lightbulb.

"Oh no," I whispered.

Immediately I sprinted to my cabin, jumped up the steps, unlocked the padlock, and swung open the door. Mosquitos were everywhere—swarming the front door and windows, hovering below the light, climbing on the ceiling, covering a mosquito net above the bed. It was a near-disaster, and for a moment I didn't know what to do and even considered calling David and asking if I could crash at his place for the night.

But I couldn't give up so easily. I created the mess and I needed to fix it. So I slammed the door, flipped off the light switch, and rushed to the end of the bed where I found my headlamp on the middle shelf. Then I turned it on, placed it over my head, gripped *Life of Pi*, and got to work.

Like a ruthless hunter, I killed without discretion. Jumping over the bed, leaping toward the ceiling, and lunging across the room, I chased down each and every insect, and smashed their delicate frames. Once I cleared the room, I unwrapped the mosquito net and spread it around the mattress. Then I washed up in the bathroom and slipped under the netting into bed. After twenty minutes of frenzied panic, I could finally relax. Maybe even pray.

With a sigh, I opened my journal and began writing. Words burst out, flowing like an open wound, spilling onto the paper. A page into my thoughts, I noticed movement from the corner of my eye. I stopped writing and looked up. The headlamp revealed nothing out of the ordinary. My belongings still sat on the two bottom shelves and the hanger contraption remained secure on the edge of the top shelf. I looked down and picked up where I left off. A moment later, another movement distracted me. My eyes darted to the second shelf. The movement hadn't been abrupt, but slow and subtle, almost like the crawl of a...*rat*.

"Ahhh," I yelled, jumping back and retracting my hands. My journal and pen flew into the air, then landed on the floor with a thud.

The rat froze. Sitting in a crouched position, it resembled a tiger stalking prey. Half its body hid behind a stack of books. The other half remained exposed. Its head slowly shifted toward me and we nearly made eye contact. Its leg muscles looked tense. Its glazy eyes reflected my headlamp. I had no doubt: this creature stole my loaf of banana bread and returned to take the coconut bread.

Like a hawk, I eyed the rat until it finally moved. It crawled around the stack of books and, for a fraction of a second, paused. Somehow I sensed it was about to take a risk. Since earlier in the day, it'd been a mystery how the creature got from the floor to the top shelf, which stood a good four feet off the ground. It became clear I'd misjudged the rat's intelligence and athleticism. With ease, it leapt on top of the books, reached an arm above its head, and pulled itself onto the top shelf. Through it all, the rat remained oblivious to the fact its prize remained impossibly out of reach.

Patiently, I watched the rat tiptoe along the edge of the shelf. Then, when it was only a few inches from the hanger contraption, I reached to the side of the bed and grasped a half-full bottle of water. Ever so slowly, I cocked my arm behind my right ear. And then with explosive force I hurled the bottle at the rat.

A millisecond before impact, the rat looked toward the makeshift weapon. I imagined its brief yet happy life flashing before its dark beady eyes. But then the unexpected happened—in a stroke of fortune, the rat tripped. So instead of taking the bottle to the head—likely causing its death, or at least a bad concussion—its plump torso received the brunt of the impact. Knocked off balance, the rat spiraled off the edge of the shelf, and as it fell through the air, its arms and legs thrashed wildly. With a thump it hit the ground.

I jumped to my feet and lunged to the end of the bed. Standing there, I could do nothing more than watch the rat claw at the floor with its wiry feet and dart away. I fell to the ground in a pushup position and scanned under the bed. The rat was nowhere to be found. It had escaped.

My arms buckled and my body collapsed—I felt defeated. But then I noticed something odd under the bed. I reached for the object and brought it toward me.

In my hand, I held a loaf of banana bread—*my* missing loaf of banana bread, the same loaf of banana bread stolen earlier in the day by the rat. I fell onto my back and started laughing. Not a giggle, but a prolonged, deep-in-the-bones belly laugh, the sort that hurts so badly you want it to stop. But it doesn't stop, and you're thankful, because it feels good to let it out.

Eventually, I sat up. Then, as silence returned to the room, the loneliness rushed back—slamming into me like a truck. And for the first time, I forced myself to admit what I feared all along: maybe no one, not even Alissa, could make my loneliness go away.

Loneliness hadn't stalked me just that day—it had stalked me for the past fifteen years. With the loss of my friends in seventh grade came an overwhelming sense of loneliness that had never really gone away. It was a sense of otherness, an understanding I didn't belong and never would.

Throughout the remainder of junior high and high school, I looked to fill that hole through friends and, especially, Adam. But no one could. I hoped a girlfriend could solve the problem, but without the courage to ask anyone out, the loneliness only grew. Over time I learned to accept it as my constant companion, my dark shadow. And in a twisted way, even though I hated it, I found myself comforted by its presence.

Only recently, with Alissa, had it come under attack. Maybe loneliness didn't have to define me. Maybe I wouldn't end up old and alone. Maybe I could love another person who loved me back—and maybe that love would change me. Not that any single person could satisfy my every longing and need, but there's power in a relationship defined by complete acceptance and love—without fault or condition. It changes everything.

In times like this, I had to ask myself why I decided to travel instead of return to DC and spend time with Alissa. Sometimes I wondered if only half of me desired intimacy.

As I sat on the floor, surrounded by dead bugs and banana bread crumbs, I finally saw how loneliness had controlled my life—and still did. It wasn't only present when I lost my friends in seventh grade and failed to date in high school. It was present when my brothers picked on me as a kid. It was present when my trust was shattered as a teenager. It was always there—as far back as four years old.

Almost everyone I cared deeply for had rejected me in one way or another—whether through betrayal or abandonment or exploitation. That's what was at the heart of my loneliness: rejection.

Throughout adolescence and early adulthood I avoided intimacy not because I feared rejection, but because I was familiar with rejection. Even though I despised the accompanying loneliness, I understood it far better than the alternative—love. And the familiar is *always* the easier path to travel. Even when it's paved with suffering and ends in isolation. So it's the path I followed.

But that doesn't mean it's the only path.

My counselor once used an illustration that stuck with me. He said when circus elephants are born, a dinky chain is placed around one of their legs. The chain restrains the tiny creatures, keeping them from wandering off and getting into trouble. Yet it also keeps them from exploring the world around them. As they grow into massive beasts, the elephants gain the strength to easily snap the chain. But they never do. Though infinitely stronger, they still believe they're under its control. So they remain stuck, never moving beyond the chain.

This was my dangling chain keeping me restrained. And I was ready to tear it off and move forward.

That came with risk, of course. Abandoning loneliness and pursuing intimacy required enormous change. Change doesn't come easy, especially after years of believing a lie. I would have to begin exposing my heart and sharing my secrets. I would have to stop protecting and hiding, and instead, offer myself without defenses. Perhaps most difficult, I would have to stop seeing myself as an outsider unworthy of affection, but fully accepted and loved.

After a while, I stood from the floor and stepped outside onto the deck. Sitting on a chair overlooking the ocean, I took a deep breath. A cool breeze brushed against me, ruffling my hair. The moon dangled close to the horizon, surrounded by a city of shining stars. A wave crashed in the distance, and as the water settled, the ocean breathed all around me.

And I knew—I just knew—I wouldn't always be alone.

8

BEFORE I LOOKED AWAY

I saw her for only a moment. Although I wanted to look again, I kept my eyes glued to the grimy road and continued walking down the dark and crowded street. When I reached the end of the block, I stopped and looked at David.

"Did you see that?" I said, pointing up the street.

He glimpsed behind his shoulder. "See what?"

"That woman," I said, shaking my head and tightening my jaw. "She unbuttoned her blouse and, well, showed me her...breasts."

He furrowed his brow. "Really?"

"Yeah."

"Back there?"

"Yes," I said, raising my voice.

"Nope. Didn't see her." He looked confused, like he didn't understand the fuss.

I inhaled deeply and exhaled. The thick evening air smelled like burning trash. "We should probably start heading back anyway."

"Yeah?"

I nodded. "It's past two and I'm getting tired."

"Alright." David looked around. "My motorcycle's back that way," he said, pointing in the direction we came.

"Oh...well maybe we can find a different route."

"Sure thing," he said, squinting his eyes and looking up and down the road. "If we make it to the waterfront, we should be able to loop around to it."

"Cool."

I followed David down the street, dodging western tourists and scantily clad Thai women. Many of the guys grasped the hand of one or two girls, heading somewhere fast. There was a look of determination in their eyes, like nothing could stop them. Restaurants and open-air clubs lined the street for blocks, overflowing with college- and middle-aged guys, almost exclusively American and European.

Inside the clubs, Thai women wearing bikinis and miniskirts paraded their bodies on small round stages or held trays and served drinks. And then there were the "ladyboys"—dancers who dressed and talked and acted like women but were actually men.

We were in the heart of Patong, a coastal city in Thailand notorious for sex tourism. It's where western men travel to live out their fantasies in anonymity. The way it worked, so I heard, was if a guy saw a particular woman he liked, he bought her a drink and she remained by his side as long as her glass remained full. She kept him company and they flirted and talked and, over time, got quite physical, as if they really liked each other.

Of course, it didn't end with drinks. If he offered cash, she almost certainly accepted and returned to his hotel.

Despite the reputation, I wanted to visit Patong and convinced David to come along. Not because I wanted to do anything crazy. But I was curious. Plenty of people visit foreign countries, stick to the family-friendly attractions, and return home with pretty pictures and stock stories. I didn't want to be one of those people. I wanted to experience every aspect of a country, even the dark underbelly, corners others try to ignore or straight-up avoid. I wanted to see if it was true what everyone said about this place.

It also helped that Patong was only an hour from the beach cabin where I'd been staying. I figured David and I could slip into the city, check it out for a few hours, then take off, unburdened and unencumbered. I quickly learned the naiveté of my expectations.

It devastated me to see women exploited. These were mothers and daughters, girls who once wanted something better for their lives, but because of abuse or poverty or brute force, felt compelled to sell their bodies. I couldn't think of anything more tragic.

And then *it* happened. While walking down the street, past clubs and bars, I saw her. She was dancing on a small circular stage in an open-air club, surrounded by hordes of drunk guys ogling her every move. She had long skinny legs and dark hair that fell to her shoulders. Her face was lean with sharp features and she had almond-shaped eyes. She was attractive, but so were most of the women.

For some reason, though, my eyes fixed onto her and I couldn't look away.

She must have noticed me watching as I walked by, because for a brief moment, our eyes locked and she flashed a smile that made me feel like she actually wanted *me*. Then seamlessly, boldly, confidently, she unbuttoned her blouse.

Before I looked away, I saw everything—her narrow waist, her flat stomach, her supple breasts, her teasing smile.

All of her.

Then it was over. In fewer than five seconds, the time it took to walk past the club, I made eye contact with a dancer and watched her undress. And the truth is, I liked it—I liked the adrenaline, I liked the endorphins, I liked the dopamine. Yet I felt awful, like I'd participated in the very activities that stained this tragic place—the exploitation and decadence.

But here's the thing: I hadn't done anything wrong, and therefore, I didn't have a reason to feel guilty. It's not like I sat below the stage, buying her drinks and offering cash. I certainly hadn't taken advantage of her. If anything, she took advantage of me. All I did was notice a beautiful woman. That was entirely natural. Regardless, a burden weighed on my soul. I felt dirty, soiled, ashamed.

After a few blocks, we reached the busy waterfront and crossed the street onto a sidewalk buffering the beach from a stream of traffic. Spread across white sand, crowds congregated around fire pits, moving their bodies to the rhythmic thump of rap music. A fire dancer swung balls of flames attached to chains, sketching figure eights and corkscrews in the air. A dozen food carts lined the sidewalk, competing for customers with signs announcing crepes and fruit smoothies. Wisps of spice-infused smoke drifted from frying pans, collecting into a cloud hanging above the carts.

"Want one?" David asked.

"Sure."

We stopped at the first cart and ordered two crepes. David picked strawberry and I went with banana. A middle-aged woman poured a thin layer of batter onto two round skillets, spread it into a circle with a small wooden scraper, and flipped it over. In swift precise movements, she sliced three strawberries with a knife and dropped them into a crepe, then repeated the process with a banana. She topped the fruit with whipped cream, folded each crepe in half, and slid them onto two paper plates.

"Strawberry," she said, extending one plate to David.

He took it and thanked her.

"Banana," she said, handing me the other plate.

"Thank you," I said.

I walked behind David, past the other food carts, and we stopped at a clearing. The tide must have been out because I only saw black and the ocean's white-noise sounded distant.

"You know," I said, between bites, "that's only the second time that's happened to me."

"What?" David asked.

"Seen a naked woman."

"Oh," he said slowly, pivoting his head. "Really?"

"Yeah."

He narrowed his eyes. "You mean in real life?"

"Yeah, in the flesh."

"Not counting the internet or movies or whatever?"

"Right, exactly. But real life is different."

"Wait," he interrupted. "In all your years, you've never stepped into a strip club or been with a girl and one thing led to another?"

"Yup. Exactly." I thought for a few seconds. "Actually, I have been inside a strip club, but I was only there to get a friend and kept my back to the stage. So I never saw anything."

David chuckled. "Okay," he said, the word escaping his mouth slowly.

"Anyway, it surprised me seeing that woman back there. You know, take her blouse off. I kinda feel bad about it."

He glanced at his crepe, took a bite, and looked at me. "Yeah, that makes sense. I wouldn't overthink it, though. It's not a big deal."

David ate the last bite of his crepe, folded the paper plate, and tossed it into a trashcan. Stuffing the rest into my mouth, I handed him my plate. He looked at me with a smirk and laughed.

"What?" I said, shielding my mouth with my free hand.

"Nothing," he said, grabbing my plate and dropping it into the trashcan. "You ready to get outta here?"

I finished chewing and then swallowed. "Yeah, let's go."

ONE AFTERNOON DURING THE SUMMER BEFORE EIGHTH GRADE, I WAS hanging out with a friend when his dad asked him to help out in the backyard. My friend took off, leaving me alone in his bedroom.

I eventually ended up in the kitchen with his mom. She was in her late thirties, a swim coach, and quite attractive. While she emptied the dishwasher, we chatted about nothing in particular. Suddenly, she looked distracted, as if remembering something important. Without a word, she walked down the hallway toward her bedroom. I didn't know if she wanted me to come along to continue our conversation, so I followed three or four steps behind, my footsteps muffled on the shag carpet.

In her bedroom, she slipped her sweatshirt over her head, tossed it onto the unmade bed, and stepped into the bathroom. Adrenaline pumped through my body. Although I only saw her back, it looked so raw. So real. So naked. I considered running back to the kitchen and pretending I hadn't seen anything.

But only seconds later, she returned to the bedroom with a t-shirt in her hand—and her body exposed. I quickly dropped my head.

"Oh, Paul," she yelled, shielding her chest while slipping the t-shirt on. "I didn't see you."

"Sorry," I murmured. "I didn't realize...I don't know what happened. I'm sorry."

"Don't worry," she said, walking past me into the hallway. "It's not a big deal."

But it was a big deal. It devastated me. I felt as though I'd done something terribly wrong, something evil and sinful. And I knew I could never tell anyone. Especially my parents.

WALKING DOWN THE SIDEWALK, I FELT AS THOUGH I'D STEPPED BACK in time to my thirteen-year-old self. Distant emotions returned and shame pounded me, multiplying the guilt about seeing the dancer take off her blouse. I couldn't explain why, but recalling that hazy memory from years before agitated something within.

Which seemed strange because I hadn't thought about it in years. In fact, I never once told anyone what happened.

Through counseling, I'd already learned shame produces secrecy, and secrecy compounds shame—it's a self-feeding cycle, growing larger and larger until it consumes like a raging fire. Without the maturity to end the cycle by betraying my instinct toward secrecy and processing it with someone I trusted, this memory took on a life of its own, transforming into something larger than the event itself. No longer was it simply about seeing my friend's mom naked. Now it reinforced a complex. Nudity and sexuality further became associated with shame. And the secrecy only increased.

The more I considered it, the more I realized this cycle went way, way back.

SOMETIME IN SIXTH GRADE, I STAYED OVERNIGHT AT A FRIEND'S HOUSE and we watched a movie on HBO. About an hour into it, there was a nude scene. Embarrassment and guilt flooded over me. I swallowed hard, trying to erase the bitterness in my mouth, but it wouldn't go away. It lingered all night, tormenting my soul.

In the morning, my friend's mom asked what movie we watched. Without guile, my friend told her. She looked surprised. "Isn't it rated R?"

My eyes fell to the floor. I knew the consequence of her question. She'd find out and tell my parents. I could see the disappointment and shock in my mom's eyes. I could hear the anger and grief in my dad's voice. I almost cried thinking about it.

A proud smile stretched across my friend's face. "Yeah."

"Did you see any...nudity?"

"Oh yeah," my friend said, laughing hard. "We saw boobs and stuff."

She shook her head. "You're not supposed to watch those sorts of movies." Then she glanced at me and smirked. "I won't say anything if you don't."

I couldn't believe my ears—she wouldn't tell my parents. I was free. But then another wave of guilt hit. I still needed to confess. But how could I let them down like that? The risk was too great. So I determined to uphold my end of the deal—to keep quiet and hope the memory faded away, disappeared into the distance.

Months later, and only weeks before starting seventh grade, my soccer team traveled to Vancouver, BC, for a tournament. All my teammates were good friends and everyone was excited to get away for a weekend. The last night, we crowded into my hotel room to celebrate, which at that age meant movies and candy. Because we were without supervision, we expected to stay up all night.

A food fight erupted the moment the movie got under-way. Popcorn and Skittles flew across the room and we were all laughing, having a great time. Then someone got ahold of the remote and began channel surfing. Everyone started yelling and hollering. I hopped off my bed to fetch the remote and someone chucked a Fig Newton at me, tagging my eye. I fell to the floor and lowered my face into my hands. My eye throbbed and, when I opened it, a black spot appeared in the corner of my vision.

As the chaos continued around me, I kept my head down and rubbed my eye, afraid I'd gone partially blind. Then the room grew silent. Dead silent—other than some odd moaning noises. I lowered my hand from my face, opened my uninjured eye, and looked at the television. That's when I saw a man and woman having sex. Adrenalin unleashed into my body and for a moment I couldn't look away—it was gross yet spectacular. Then the guilt hit.

"Come on," I said, standing to my feet while keeping my back to the TV. "Turn it to the movie." I blinked twice. My eye still hurt and a black spot still blocked part of my vision.

"Shut up, Perkins," someone shouted. "This is what we're watching now."

"Yeah," a few people said, followed by scattered laughs.

I returned to the floor and tried to avoid looking at the TV. But I didn't want my friends to think I was different. So I pretended to enjoy it. I laughed when they laughed and emulated their stunned expressions. But I hated every moment. I hated the weird noises. I hated the strained faces. I hated the bodies smashing together. And most of all, I hated being stuck in that room, surrounded by friends, fascinated and uncomfortable and consumed with guilt.

I eventually worked up the courage to tiptoe out of the room. Sitting in the hallway, I watched the black spot gradually vanish from my vision and hoped everything I'd seen and heard would go away too. But it didn't; the memories remained, as did the guilt weighing upon me.

That's exactly how I felt walking down the street in Patong. It made me wonder how I made a connection between sexuality and shame in the first place. I hadn't been born with that association—in fact, my earliest memory of sexuality involves curiosity, not shame. Somehow I'd picked it up along the way.

Actually, I knew exactly how. As much as I wanted to deny it, as much as I wanted to run from it, as much as I wanted to bury it underground along with all my rotting memories, I had to face the truth.

It began with what happened when I was four years old. A single mother from church asked if her son, Jamie, who was also four, could stay with my family for several months. She was undergoing treatment for multiple sclerosis and didn't have the energy to care for him. My parents, of course, said yes.

Instantly Jamie and I became best friends. We did everything together, even sharing a bedroom. I loved having someone around who treated me well—someone I could play with without fear of antagonism or aggression. Even more, his presence deflected some of my brothers' teasing. I could finally let down my guard a bit. It was an all-around win.

But then one afternoon our friendship forever changed. While playing in our bedroom, Jamie told me to do something that didn't make sense. I told him no, but somehow he convinced me. I don't remember exactly what happened—the memories are blurry like faded snapshots, and I can't fully piece them together. But I do remember my dad's response when he found out. Never before had I seen him so upset. And it scared me—more than I'd been scared in my short life.

He sat me down and told me to tell him exactly what happened. But as I looked into his eyes, I couldn't admit the truth. Not because I was afraid of him—I knew he loved me and would never hurt me. I was afraid because my dad was my hero. The one person in this world I admired most. Above all else, I feared his disappointment. I didn't want to let him down. So I simply responded, "What did Jamie say?"

He continued probing, but every time he asked another question, I responded in the same way—"What did Jamie say?" Eventually, he stopped asking the same questions over and over. By the end of it, I was broken. Something inside shattered and I had to keep it hidden. No one could ever know. It was a heavy burden to carry, a heavy secret to hold.

That's the weight I lugged around for the remainder of my childhood. In the back of my mind, I feared people finding out— my friends, my brothers, even strangers. I was convinced that I, and I alone, had done terrible things that could never be forgotten, and at any point they could be uncovered.

At the same time, life went on. Jamie left and everything returned to the way it was before. Yet inside I'd changed. Now I understood there was something wrong with sexuality. Of course, that's not what my parents told me. In fact, they taught what most Christian parents teach: sexuality is something to be explored only within the context of marriage. Even in their own relationship, my parents demonstrated healthy sexuality— affection, passion, love, and respect.

None of that mattered, though. Shame had already convinced me that sexuality was dangerous and wrong and needed to remain hidden. My parents' efforts to protect my brothers and me only reinforced this lie.

For instance, while watching movies as a family, my mom had a tendency to overreact every time a man and woman became intimate. She'd jump from the couch, race to the TV, and shield the screen with a pillow or blanket or even her body, all while screaming for us to look away and my dad to fast-forward the video. If we were at a theater, she'd cover our eyes with her hands or a jacket or her purse. I understood she was merely trying to protect us, only reacting to her maternal instinct. But still.

For his part, my dad filtered our computers and televisions to guard our family from pornography. But the thing is, I never wanted to look at porn as a kid. It scared me, and my dad's persistence only reinforced these fears—and made me wonder if he had a problem himself.

Nothing my parents said or did during this period was necessarily wrong. In fact, I never once questioned their sincerity or motivation. They were simply doing their best in a world seemingly at war with their values. And I don't doubt it was to my benefit that as a child my parents protected me from pornography.

There's a consequence to instilling fear in a child, though. While it might have led to the response they wanted, it didn't produce a confident and assertive kid with concrete boundaries. Instead, it created a boy prone to shame, afraid to disappoint, and willing to do almost anything to hide the truth when it stood at odds with what was "right."

Coming face to face with my parents' imperfections was deeply painful. I never wanted to critique their parenting because I love and respect them more than anyone on earth. The last thing I ever wanted was to hurt them or let them down or make them think they were anything other than the best parents. But I also recognized this fear of disappointing them, this fear of causing them pain, was the root of my reflex toward secrecy.

If I ever wanted freedom from these memories, if I ever wanted healing from guilt and shame, if I ever wanted to abandon my impulse to hide, if I ever wanted to forgive my mom and dad, I had to confront the truth of my past. And the truth is, my parents unwittingly hurt me.

My dad in particular created a lasting wound when he confronted me about what happened with Jamie. He approached me more as a prosecutor rather than a father. Although I now recognize he probably wasn't so much angry as he was fearful, at the time I didn't know the difference. I was too young to understand. All I knew was I had disappointed my dad, the one man on this planet who really mattered, and I had done just about the worst thing possible. The only way to cope with that weight was to hide myself away. And so I did. I hid in a corner—where every day since, a part of me has remained.

So when I was eleven and saw a naked woman while watching a movie at a friend's house, and when I was twelve and saw porno with my soccer team, and when I was thirteen and saw my friend's mom take her sweatshirt off, these were not exciting coming-of-age experiences. They were devastating blows to my identity. They rattled me to the core. And they too needed to stay secret.

By hiding these memories, though, by burying them deep underground, they had never really gone away. They had always been there, tugging at my soul, pulling me back, dragging me down, even as I grew into an adult. So when the dancer slipped off her blouse, it wasn't simply me, a grown man, who saw it. There was also a little boy, afraid and ashamed, frozen in time by trauma and pain, standing by my side.

My eyes felt heavy by the time David and I reached the crowded parking lot. I followed at a distance as we wove through a tangled-mess of scooters and motorcycles. When I reached David's bike, he was already sitting on it with the engine idling.

"You alright?" he asked, concern evident in his eyes.

"Yeah," I said, nodding my head. "I think I'll be okay."

"You still thinking about what you saw back there?"

I hesitated. "Yeah." I felt bad admitting it, knowing he probably thought I was making something of nothing. But I didn't want to hide anymore.

He looked at me for moment. Then he said, "It's not your fault, Paul."

"Thanks, bro. I appreciate that."

Sitting behind David, I leaned my hands against the back rest and took a deep breath. The bike lunged forward, and we quickly drove out of the parking lot and onto a coastal road. As we climbed a hill, I looked over my shoulder at the city one final time. Lights surrounded by evening darkness sparkled in the distance and the moon's light reflected off the still ocean.

Then a headlight appeared behind us at the bottom of the hill. It slowly grew larger until a motorcycle pulled even with us. A man with a helmet over his head sat in front and a Thai woman sat close behind, her hands wrapped around his waist. She wore high-heels, a short skirt, and a t-shirt. She glanced at me with an air of confidence, as though she never once doubted the life she lived.

But before she looked away, I saw through it all. She wasn't so much a woman, but a child—alone and afraid. I sensed the wounds she had suffered growing up, the abandonment and abuse, the unnecessary guilt and consuming shame, and how it had molded her over the years, forming the woman she became, explaining why she sat on the back of a bike with a man she didn't know, why she sold her body and also her soul.

Somehow I knew all she ever wanted, and still hoped to find, was someone to love her, and accept her, and tell her none of it was her fault. All the pain, all the suffering, all the abuse—it wasn't her fault. She'd only been a kid, a victim, and in so many ways she was still that same little girl. Although she'd made mistakes over the years, she'd only been acting out of the pain of her past. Reacting to what she'd suffered. But she didn't need to continue living in that place. She had the power to once and for all move beyond it.

Then I realized what I only suspected about this woman I knew about myself. What the child within needed—what *I* needed—was what David had just provided. The soft reassurance that none of the pain, none of the suffering, none of the shame was any of my fault.

It wasn't my fault what Jamie did to me. It wasn't my fault my dad responded without the care and sensitivity I needed. It wasn't my fault I saw nudity at my friend's house, and porn with my soccer team, and my friend's mom shirtless. It wasn't my fault when as a teenager someone I trusted exploited me. None of it was my fault. Though I had done plenty I regretted and even bore responsibility for seeking protection in secrecy, I'd really been acting out of the pain of my past. And that wasn't my fault.

Only when I accepted that could the little boy turn around and step away from the corner. Only then could I wrap my arms around him and let him go on his way. And only then could I finally reject the lie I believed so many years ago that sexuality is shameful and what is shameful must be hidden.

A moment later, the motorcycle passed, and in no time at all, it was only a small red light in the distance. And then it was gone.

9

ONE PEDAL AT A TIME

Sitting in an open-air public bus, I pictured myself rolling into the small town of Kanchanaburi, finding a quaint hotel on the bank of the beautiful Khwae Yai River, and surveying bike rental shops until I found my ride for the day. I envisioned mounting a brand new 21-speed and setting off on a leisurely trek through rolling hills and ancient villages. A smooth trail would guide my journey and a soft breeze would keep me cool. I would stop to photograph breathtaking views and treat myself to a refreshing, ice-cold beverage.

A few hours into the ride, I would pull up to a restaurant and enjoy local Thai cuisine, my taste buds dancing in bliss. As the afternoon transitioned into evening, the cloudless sky would fade from baby blue to florescent pink, then burst bright orange and violet red—the sky blossoming before my eyes. In that moment, my mind would clear of every confusing thought. Every painful memory and regret would blur to the backdrop, forever forgotten.

As darkness overtook the sky and stars sparkled overhead, I would stroll back to town, enjoy a warm shower, grab a bite to eat, and return to my hotel room. With a good book in hand, I would take a seat overlooking the rushing river and read until my mind began drifting.

An abrupt stop ended my daydream. A handful of Thais jumped out of their seats and pushed their way down the aisle. Gazing out the window, I searched for a clue to indicate where we'd stopped. A line of public buses—some green, others orange, a few red—were parked beside us, passengers funneling in and out of each. Decorative Thai script tagged their front windshields and muffled voices from outside blended into a hum.

I leaned forward to look out the opposite window and saw an oversized charter, likely retrofitted with AC, reclining chairs, and TVs. Only tourists are willing to pay the extra cash to travel in luxury. Locals—and budget-minded westerners like myself—elect to get around by public buses outfitted with the bare minimum: hard metal seats with quarter-inch padding, a near constant squeaking of loose bolts against rusted metal, and a single oscillating fan in back that, if operable, contributes to the wind-tunnel-like effect of the informal open window policy. It wasn't too bad, although the lack of English speakers made it tough to get around.

"Are we here?" I mumbled, scanning a half-empty bus of Thais slumbering in their seats despite the all-consuming heat. "Is this Kanchanaburi?"

No one responded. I looked at the man beside me, an elderly monk dressed in a flowing orange robe, and gently tapped his boney shoulder. His eyes slipped open and his chin rose. When he saw my face, his mouth lifted into a toothless grin and he muttered something unintelligible.

"Kanchanaburi?" I asked with my best Thai accent.

He nodded while uttering an affirmative moan. As soon as the noise escaped his mouth, his eyelids rolled back over his eyeballs and his chin sank toward his chest.

"Thank you," I whispered, then I gently squeezed by him, careful not to step on his robe or bump his delicate frame. I grabbed my backpack from the aisle, slung it over my shoulder, and trotted off the bus into the sweltering afternoon sunlight—eager to turn my daydream into reality.

A WEEK EARLIER I HAD SAID GOODBYE TO DAVID IN PHUKET AND SET off on a thousand-mile journey to the northernmost tip of Thailand. Stopping along the way, I explored villages and cities, and met locals and fellow travelers. Sometimes I rented a motor scooter and roamed the streets and countryside. Other times I set out on a bike with no destination in mind. Each day or two I moved on.

The more I traveled, the more comfortable I felt alone and the more I appreciated, even savored, going without a plan. I sensed it drawing me out, giving me confidence, and teaching me assertiveness. Never before had I been so independent.

That's not to say I hadn't exhibited self-reliance or self-sufficiency when I went to college, or moved across the country to DC, or interviewed for jobs, or walked into the White House day after day, or persevered through law school. I obviously had—only in a different sort of way.

Those are worlds in which I'm comfortable. The rules are clear. The protocol is laid out. My role is defined. Each simply required more of the qualities I'd already honed—discipline, focus, hard work, and drive. Those were the keys to success.

It's different when traveling alone in a foreign country and immersing yourself in a new culture—not avoiding the differences by staying at fancy resorts and riding charter buses or hiring drivers, but living like the locals. Taking rickshaws. Staying at cheap hotels. Mixing it up with strangers. Eating street food. Observing everyday life. Going where the people go.

Nothing about that world is comfortable or familiar. Everything is different. And discipline, focus, hard work, and drive, instead of assets, are often counterproductive. So my cherished routine, my structured schedule, my need for productivity and efficiency, my demand for comfort and control—out the window. As foreign as sitting in the back of a bicycle rickshaw.

The fact that everything hadn't gone as planned would have freaked me out in the past. I disliked nothing more than surprise and uncertainty. But recently I had come to embrace the unplanned and unexpected. I sensed God using every experience, especially those I didn't orchestrate, to mold me.

I also found myself with added confidence in my relationship with Alissa. For years I struggled to see myself as the type of guy a woman would want to date. Even though I achieved success at work and in school, I didn't feel strong or confident around women but instead insecure and skittish.

I'm sure my self-image made me less attractive—it certainly affected how I acted around girls. I rarely asked girls out, and when I did, I treated it as a friendly chill session. Not a romantic date. And the times I liked a girl, it usually didn't last long, because any fluctuation of feeling or emotion threw me into a panic. I would just bail.

There were girls I liked for years but never asked out, and girls I liked for days to whom I spilled my heart. There were girls

I dated but didn't like, and girls I liked but refused to date. Then there were the girls from long ago who I couldn't forget—crushes from high school and college, relationships I failed to pursue, girls I tried to rescue. I nurtured each into a precious memory, a talisman of sorts that kept me from living in the moment and seeing what stood in front of me.

These are not the qualities of a man but a boy. And I knew it. How, I wondered, could I take care of a wife and kids if I didn't feel stable, secure, and confident?

Perhaps this immaturity is why it took me so long to take my relationship with Alissa seriously. I knew she wasn't the type of girl who messed around. And I didn't know if I had what it took to date a real woman.

Those days seemed long past.

LOOKING AROUND, I NOTICED A SCATTERING OF BICYCLE RICKSHAWS parked in the shade of a giant tree. Drivers reclined in their backseats, napping through the hottest hour of the day. As I walked toward them, my flip-flops shuffled across the dust-caked concrete. One of the drivers must have heard me because he lifted his head. A soft smile animated his saggy face and, as if coming to life, he sprang out of his rickshaw and struck the ground with a thump.

At first I thought he hurt himself with the landing. He bent at the waist and looked like he was about to crumple into a pile of bones. But then he straightened up and smiled again, display-ing a mouthful of missing teeth. "Welcome," he shouted, patting the backseat. Plumes of dust burst into the air. "I take you hotel, you no worry. Come now."

At the sound of his voice, several drivers looked his way. Some appeared to chuckle. I figured it was because they didn't think he had the strength to pull me. Clearly the guy was past his prime, and I too wondered if he was up for the job. But I wanted to give him a chance. I wanted to believe he could do it.

I tossed my backpack onto the thinly padded backseat, jarring the rickshaw, then hopped in beside it. I fished out a heavily-marked guidebook and flipped to a map of Kanchanaburi. "Can you take me here?" I asked, pointing to a small house icon next to the Khwae Yai River. The colorful description of a quaint guesthouse made it sound like an exclusive lodge on a lush river. While the cheapest hotels were normally bare-boned, this one seemed like a diamond in the rough. And although I'd stopped caring about western comforts, sleeping on a soft bed and showering under warm water sounded too wonderful to pass up.

The man studied the map, tilting his head and narrowing his bloodshot eyes. "Here?"

I nodded and said, "What do you think?"

"Okay," the man said with a sigh.

I shut the guidebook and placed it inside my backpack. Then I reclined in the tattered seat and braced for the rickshaw to take off toward the destination. But it didn't. Instead of hopping on the bicycle seat and pedaling, the man gripped the handlebars and began pushing. Over uneven pavement and scattered potholes, the rickshaw crawled forward one step at a time, my body jolting from each bump. His pushing quickly grew unsteady and his breathing labored. I considered getting off the rickshaw, patting him on the shoulder, and sending him back to the shade. But I didn't want to humiliate him, and I still wanted to give him a chance. So I remained seated, encouraging him with words I hoped he understood.

After a while, we rolled onto a lightly trafficked road cutting through town. With a deep exhale and loud groan, the man tossed his right leg over the sweat-stained seat and forced his body onto the bicycle. Standing up, his wiry legs quivered and his toes clinched the pedals as he shifted his bodyweight from one side of the bike to the other. One pedal at a time, we inched toward the hotel.

We remained on that road for what seemed like an hour, occasionally joined by a truck or bus surging past us with a blaring horn, gurgling engine, and wake of dust. Listening to the man's near-constant moan, I wondered if perhaps I'd placed too much confidence in him. Maybe he wasn't up to the task. Maybe I should have gone with someone else. But what could I do? Other than pedal myself, which would have been the ultimate demoralization, I could only hope for the best. So I did—I prayed he would make it home to his family that night.

Eventually, we turned onto an alley parallel to a narrow waterway.

"Is that the river?" I asked.

The driver stopped pedaling and turned his head toward me. A smile lifted his face, exposing deep wrinkles from the corners of his eyes to his temples. "Mae," he said, followed by a gasp for air. "Nam," he continued, pausing again. "Khwae Yai."

"Oh." I unzipped my backpack and fumbled for my guidebook. "The map made it look so much bigger." I flipped through the book until I found the map of Kanchanaburi, then dog-eared the corner of the page in case I needed to return to it.

"Beautiful, no?"

"Yeah. In a way, I guess." I shut the guidebook and locked my eyes on the smaller-than-expected river.

A minute later, the man said, "Okay."

"Okay?"

"We're here."

To my left, a rickety stairway led down to the river. Weeds dressed the railing and a few boards looked rotten. Below the stairway sat a crumbling structure. A narrow walkway connected that building to a chain of shacks floating on the swamp-like water. Down the road, a concrete bridge crossed the river. A motor rickshaw raced across it, emitting the sound of a lawnmower and leaving a trail of grey exhaust.

"This is the hotel?"

The man turned around and looked at me. Then he nodded. Sweat dripped from his forehead and onto the dusty road, staining it with drops like blood.

"Alright…" I said, hesitating to step out of the rickshaw. The place looked like an abandoned row of shacks. Not a palatial guesthouse.

"Go and look," he said, pointing at the stairway. "I wait."

"Okay." I stepped out of the rickshaw and crossed the street. Halfway down the stairway, I stopped. Something about this place didn't feel right. It also smelled bad. So I turned around and headed back to the rickshaw.

Sitting on his bike with a cigarette between his lips, the man stared at me with a smirk. "No like?" he asked, smoke seeping from his mouth, twisting above his head.

I laughed softly. "No like."

After climbing into the rickshaw, I pulled out my guidebook and showed him another budget hotel nearby. "How about this one?"

"No," he said, waving his hand. "Your book rubbish. I take you somewhere nice." He stood on a pedal and, shifting his weight to the other pedal, nudged us forward.

"Are you sure? This hotel sounds pretty good."

He turned and looked at me. "Trust me." Then he continued pedaling.

Sitting back, I took a deep breath and watched the man's body straining as he took me to an unknown hotel. The sudden turn of events left me flustered. The thing is, I'd always been a planner, setting everything from life goals to daily schedules. Even as a kid I kept to a routine. As an adult, I'd become a machine. In part out of necessity, but also because I valued control. While this quality made me effective, I'd already learned it didn't help much while traveling.

But I was beginning to wonder if my need for control did more harm than good in my normal, everyday life as well. Perhaps embracing uncertainty and abandoning expectations worked as a lifestyle—not just a travel mind-set.

As I'd seen, only when I abandoned my plans, all my expectations and daydreams, did life get interesting. Otherwise I ended up interfering with God's plans.

At the end of the day, that's the life I wanted. I didn't want to hold so tightly to my agenda that I missed God's bigger plan. I didn't want to blindly follow my daydreams past beauty in front of me. I didn't want to fix onto a distant dream and ignore the moment-by-moment adventures around me.

Instead, I wanted to open myself to God's often-mysterious design. I wanted to embrace life, whatever it looked like, wherever it led. I wanted to see every moment as a gift, bursting with meaning and potential. That required releasing control, tossing my plans, and opening myself to the possibility that God might be up to something entirely different.

Before I knew it, we were cruising along a road bustling with activity. Shops and restaurants lined both sides of the street. Tourists strolled on the sidewalks. Bicycle rickshaws rode by in both directions. Through a clearing, I saw the river—no longer thin and shallow, but wide and deep. Down the road, I noticed a blue sign that read, "Star Guest House."

"There," the rickshaw driver said, pointing at the sign with his left hand. His right hand tightly grasped the handlebar as the muscles in his forearm twitched from exhaustion. His legs trembled with each successive rotation. When we reached the hotel, he resigned himself to the seat, bringing the rickshaw to a rolling stop. Then he took a deep breath and exhaled loudly. "Here."

"You're amazing," I said. I felt like giving the man a hug, but I didn't want to crush him. I leapt onto the pavement with my backpack over my shoulder. "Wait here. I'll be right back."

As I walked down the hotel's stone-covered driveway, tall yellow flame trees provided shaded relief from the sun. The driveway opened into a garden surrounded by seven white-washed rooms with tile patios. Several people reclined in chairs reading books, and a couple sat around an iron table enjoying a bottle of red wine. It looked like paradise.

At the front desk, a tall man greeted me with a smile. "Welcome."

"Thanks," I said. "Do you have a room available?"

He nodded. "Yes, sir. We have one remaining."

"Perfect. I'll take it." I reached into my pocket to get cash, then remembered the rickshaw driver. "Hold on a minute. I've gotta take care of something."

I took my time walking back, enjoying the surroundings of my new home for the next couple of days. I strolled past the garden, by the people reclining in chairs and reading, past the couple sipping on red wine, past the white-washed rooms and stone patios, past the yellow flame trees, and finally down the driveway.

At the street, I crossed to where I got off the rickshaw a few minutes earlier. But the man wasn't there—he and his rickshaw were gone. I scanned the street, searching for him among the crowd, but didn't see him anywhere. Then I wandered down the block, examining each rickshaw on the side of the road. If I saw him, even at a distance, I would have run after him until I caught up. But I never did find him.

I didn't understand why the man left without getting paid. Maybe he thought I forgot about him. Maybe he thought I blamed him for the earlier mishap. Or maybe he didn't want to wait. But the man seemed patient and his grasp of English was good enough to comprehend what I said about returning. He just left.

Sighing, I lowered my backpack to the ground and rested my hands on my hips. As I looked down the busy street, I imagined the old man hopping onto his bicycle and riding forward one pedal at a time. I was disappointed. I wanted to thank him for all he'd done to get me to a hotel. I wanted to make sure he felt okay after that strenuous ride. I wanted him to know how much I appreciated him. I wanted to congratulate him on a job well done.

Then, in the back of my mind, I wondered if perhaps I'd misjudged the man. What if he left because he didn't care about getting paid? Maybe for him, the payment was in helping me out—and proving to himself, and his skeptical buddies, that he still had it in him. And he certainly did. Without his assistance, I would've been stuck in a decrepit hotel trying to live out an unrealistic daydream. But because of him, I'd abandoned that fantasy and stepped into a day without plans or expectations.

I liked that idea far better than the alternative. I suspected there was more truth to it as well. With that, I turned around and returned to Star Guest House.

10

DARKNESS ALL AROUND

My eyes opened to darkness all around. The faint sound of crickets pierced a fan's hum. A breeze brushed against my legs, slowly climbed my body until it reached my chest, then worked its way back to my feet. I kicked a sheet off my legs and leaned against a metal bedframe. Across the room, a narrow window looked onto a swamp surrounding the standalone room. A clock next to the bed displayed the time in dim green lines. 5:00 *a.m.*

I swung my feet off the bed and onto the concrete floor. Trying to stand, I fell backwards, then made it on the second try. I felt hungover—my eyes stung, my stomach turned, my head pounded. And worst of all, my heart ached.

I'd been traveling alone for the past few weeks, enjoying myself but also feeling the effects of isolation. From Kanchanaburi, I visited the ancient town of Sukhothai, then headed to Chiang Mai. After a week motor-scootering around the city's narrow streets and historic wats, I traveled to Pai, a small town near the border of Burma, where I played with an elephant named Hallel. Then I made my way to Chiang Rai.

Although the loneliness weighed upon me, it's not what crushed me the night before. What kept me up all night, panicked and on the verge of tears, was my relationship with Alissa. Lately things had grown even more serious. Our emails overflowed with emotion, and our Skype sessions lasted hours. We both recognized what was happening—we were falling in love.

But the closeness also raised an issue I hadn't anticipated. Over email the day before, Alissa told me she needed to share some details about her past, stuff she thought I should know before we moved forward. She wanted to wait until we were together in India, though, so she could tell me face to face.

My stomach dropped when I read her words. Not because I feared Alissa's past. Honestly, it didn't faze me. I could handle almost anything. What worried me was revealing my own.

I'd never before told a woman what happened to me as a teenager. In fact, I'd only told a few people. It's one thing to tell a friend or counselor, someone who would accept me no matter what. It's entirely different to tell the woman I hoped to one day marry. The stakes were infinitely higher. The prospect of rejection felt real, almost inevitable.

Deep down, I feared Alissa's response. She seemed accepting, but everyone has a limit. And this, I suspected, would smash through it. It would simply be too much to stomach.

That's not to say I planned to keep it from her forever. I just hoped to avoid it a while longer, at least until we exchanged our first "I love you" or got engaged. Waiting, though, was no longer an option. I couldn't continue avoiding it. In India, I too needed to disclose my past.

As I stepped into the bathroom, the recurring question echoed in my mind. How could I possibly tell Alissa about the worst night of my life—the night Adam abused me?

I was only fourteen. He was thirty-four.

With my eyes latched, I flipped on the ceiling light. Through my eyelids, I sensed a florescent glow radiating above. I thought about turning the light back off and returning to bed—finding refuge in sleep. Placing a finger onto the light switch, I pressed the plastic knob halfway down. Then I remembered why I couldn't hide for another hour or two. I needed to get back to Bangkok to catch a flight to India.

Slowly, I opened my eyes—and immediately brightness flooded my sight. I tried to shield the light with my hands, but it didn't do any good. I stepped in front of the sink, lowered my hands onto the light-brown countertop, and leaned toward a rusted mirror. Thin lines stretched across my forehead and a wrinkle divided the ridge of my nose. My squinting eyes looked swollen and bloodshot, distracting from the green-blue blend encircling my pupils. Dark hair dangled past my narrow nose on both sides of my unshaven face. I took a deep breath, filling my lungs with stale air, then exhaled.

Under a stream of cold water I washed my hands. After inserting my contacts, I quickly washed my face and brushed my teeth, then dried off with a faded-grey towel. Carrying my toiletry bag, I walked out of the bathroom and turned on a bedside lamp.

A navy blanket rested on the floor. At the end of the bed, a sheet laid tangled in a ball. A flattened, sweat-stained pillow was lodged between the corner of the wall and the metal bedframe. A fan on the floor pointed at the bed, oscillating back and forth.

In front of the window, I packed my backpack, then changed into a pair of unwashed clothes and stepped into my flip-flops. Standing by the door with my backpack strapped around my body, I glanced at the bed once again and sighed.

I'd spent hours tossing and turning. Fears and insecurities ran through my mind. Countless times I tried to silence the voices and ask for God's help—for mercy on my soul and peace of mind, for sleep to come and dreams to arrive. But my words were too quiet to rise above the noise.

As I studied the chaotic scene, I wondered why God hadn't answered my prayers last night. Why hadn't he rescued me from despair? Why hadn't he put an end to my racing thoughts? Why hadn't he given me the reassurance I needed?

Then a deeper question surfaced. Why didn't God protect me that night when I was fourteen? Why didn't he storm into my bedroom and throw Adam onto the street? Why did he even let Adam enter my life in the first place?

I wanted to believe in God's goodness and love, but I had a hard time seeing it in light of what I'd been through. It felt hollow and empty. Couldn't he have done something? Couldn't he have kept me from harm? Couldn't he have rescued me?

It would've been easy to stop it at the beginning. When Adam first entered my life, I was a happy-go-lucky, ten-year-old kid. He and my brothers were friends, and after only a few brief interactions, he took on hero status. He was a *cool* adult—fun and smart and, most importantly, interested in me. Occasionally my brothers let me tag along when they hung out with him, but it wasn't until I turned twelve that we began spending time alone.

By that time I'd grown into a moody adolescent, and I felt the strain of friendships pulling apart. When they eventually unraveled and I found myself lonely and isolated, Adam was there for me. He listened and talked. He trusted and accepted me. He made me feel good, giving me gifts, driving me around in his sports car, taking me out to eat. And he provided the one thing I wanted more than anything—a sense I mattered.

But he couldn't leave it at that. He couldn't just be a mentor helping me through tough times. He had to twist it. So what began as a friendship slowly morphed into something different. And then late one night he crossed the line.

I wish I could say our friendship ended that night. But it didn't. What was I going to do, tell him to leave? I needed Adam more than ever. My old friends had abandoned me, and though I'd made new friends, it was only a matter of time before they rejected me too. I couldn't risk losing Adam. I couldn't risk being alone. And that meant ignoring what happened.

At the same time, our friendship changed after that night— perhaps because I refused to do what he ultimately wanted. Before, Adam was positive and uplifting. He encouraged me to stay away from drugs, he empathized with my loneliness, he showered me with attention. After that night ended, though, his kindness did too. Suddenly his attitude turned antagonistic, even cruel. He often made fun of me, calling me gay, or short, or uptight, or too religious, or whatever other supposed putdown popped into his mind.

Rarely did I push back. Instead, I took it. For years I took it. Which I guess isn't surprising if you think about it. I had a long history of appeasement and acquiescence, minimization and self-deception, secrecy and shame. So despite the cruelty and abuse, Adam and I remained friends. Even after I graduated from high school and went off to college, graduated from college and moved to DC, our friendship remained.

But after months of counseling and processing with my closest friends, I worked up the courage to abandon him. When he texted me in the middle of my cross-country move from DC to Oregon, I responded by telling him the way he treated me as a kid was really messed up and we could no longer be friends. And though sending that message brought relief, it didn't do much else—the pain, the sadness, the anger, the embarrassment, the humiliation, the guilt, the shame. It all remained.

And somehow I was supposed to tell Alissa.

With resignation, I stepped outside, closed the door behind me, and walked down the dock as creaks trailed my every footstep. A crescent moon floated above the horizon and a chorus of critters prepared to welcome the new day. In the swamp surrounding my room, blades of grass reached into the sky and lily pads floated on the water's surface. I passed several rooms and climbed a dozen steps. Then I left my key in a basket behind the front desk and made my way up the driveway toward the main road.

At the edge of the driveway I stopped. Normally the road bustled with activity—auto and bicycle rickshaws filled the street, tourists and locals flooded the sidewalk, and businesses sold t-shirts and other trinkets. It was a picture of vibrancy and life. But that was during the day—not just after five o'clock in the morning. Now it appeared lifeless. No people. No bicycles. No rickshaws.

Catching my flight to India depended upon catching a 5:30 a.m. bus from Chiang Rai to Chiang Mai. If I missed the bus, I would miss the train from Chiang Mai to Bangkok. If I missed the train, I would miss the flight from Bangkok to India. And that could set off a chain reaction I didn't want to imagine. The rest of my trip hinged upon getting on that bus in the next fifteen minutes.

I looked up and down the block, but didn't see anything hopeful. Trash littered the street and a stray dog scampered by on the sidewalk. Then in the distance, I spotted three auto rickshaws in a dirt parking lot, and I raced over to them.

At the first rickshaw, I poked my head through the passenger window but didn't see anyone. The second rickshaw was also empty. As I neared the final rickshaw, I lightened my steps and tiptoed to the driver's side. Then I looked through the window— a man with short dark hair and a bushy mustache was sprawled across the front bucket seat.

"Hello," I whispered, stepping back in case he woke up angry and I needed to bolt.

The man didn't move. Not seeing another option, I reached through the window and nudged his shoulder. "Hello," I said again, this time louder.

Without moving, the man's left eye popped open, darted around—side to side, up and down—and locked onto me. A second later, it closed.

"Wake up," I shouted. "My bus leaves in thirteen minutes." I prayed for the man to open his eye again or at least rustle around. But he didn't move. "Please. I'll pay double."

He still didn't move. So I dropped my head, turned around, and headed to the sidewalk. There's nothing worse than hopelessness—the sense that nothing you do matters. Like tossing a pebble into a frozen pond, you make no impact at all. I had no sense of direction and no idea how to get where I needed to go. I'd given up—surrendered to missing my flight and ruining the rest of my trip.

With my eyes fixed on the ground, I passed through an intersection, stepped onto a sidewalk, and paused—because I heard something. I raised my head and before my eyes a red Jeep drove out of a hotel parking lot and pulled in front of me. Then it stopped between the sidewalk and the road, blocking my path forward. Its headlights pointed at a heap of tangled bushes across the street. I thought about waving my arms, rushing at the vehicle, shouting for help—anything to get the driver's attention. But I didn't move. I only watched, waiting for the Jeep to pull into the road and drive away.

Then a shadow inside moved. I stepped forward and, squinting my eyes, peered through the passenger window. It was too dark to make anything out other than the outline of a person. The shadow reached toward the passenger door and grabbed ahold of something. A moment later the window cracked open. Then I heard the most beautiful words in all my life.

"Do you need ride?"

"Yes," I shouted.

In a single movement, I lunged at the Jeep, opened the door, and jumped inside. While buckling my seatbelt, I looked up and, for the first time, saw the driver.

She was a ladyboy. I'd seen many ladyboys in Patong— dancing on stages, serving drinks, even walking down the street holding hands with western men, probably on their way to hotels for the night. I quickly put two and two together. This ladyboy was likely leaving a hotel after sleeping with a man.

"My name Siriporn," she said with a smile. Her effeminate voice seemed to float from her lips.

"I'm Paul."

"Where you go?"

"Well, I'm trying to get to Chiang Mai, but I'm having a hard time finding the bus to take me there."

"Oh yes, I take you now."

I breathed a sigh of relief. "Really? You know where it is?"

She nodded with excitement. "Yes. Of course."

Siriporn pulled the Jeep onto the street and accelerated down the road. As she drove, I watched with curiosity. A two-inch scar stretched across her right cheek and the corners of her front teeth were chipped. Her hair, flat and dark, fell just below her ears, and she wore a miniskirt and tight shirt that showed off her stomach. She had soft facial features and a slight Adam's apple. I figured she was in her early twenties, maybe younger.

"Are you from…Amer-i-ka?" she asked.

I nodded. "Yup."

"And you travel…for fun?"

I chuckled softly. "Yeah, I guess so."

"By yourself?"

"All alone."

She shook her head and smiled. "You're so…lucky. What you see?"

"Well, last month I was in Indonesia, this month I've traveled around Thailand, and tonight I'm flying to India for a month. Assuming I make this bus."

Her jaw dropped and she swung her eyes onto me. "Wow, that is so…adventurous."

I shrugged. "It's alright. I've had a good time so far."

Siriporn eased on the brake and stopped at a stop sign. Then she drove through the intersection and onto an empty four lane highway. Once we picked up speed, she glanced at me and shook her head.

"No," she said, followed by a short laugh. "Not just alright. What you do is—" she paused, struggling to find the word—"amazing. You must be—how do I say?—brave."

My eyes widened a bit. "Thanks. I hope that's true." After a moment, "But I don't always feel like it."

Siriporn shifted her eyes onto me. "Maybe no feel it. But you are, Paul." She lifted a finger and poked my chest. "You *are* brave."

"Okay," I said bashfully. "Thanks, I guess."

"An adventure," she said loudly, tossing her hand out the window. "You are living a great adventure."

Watching Siriporn, I wondered if the words she spoke weren't just her own. Maybe, in a mystical way, they were God's words too.

My eyes moved off Siriporn and onto the sky's transition from grey to light. Then I looked back at Siriporn. With an arm dangling out the window, her hand glided through the air. I admired the exuberance despite all she'd been through—and I imagined she had a past filled with pain and abuse. She just seemed happy to be alive. Maybe that should always be enough.

"Thanks," I finally said. "I hope you're right."

Siriporn laughed softly. "I am."

I glanced away from Siriporn and watched the morning sky come to life. As pink streaks bled across the periwinkle sky and cirrus clouds radiated the sun's golden glow, I thought again about my endless spiral of doubts and questions the night before. Instead of a suffocating weight, though, I sensed a strengthening of my soul, a lifting of my spirit. And I wondered if maybe I could tell Alissa, even if it meant rejection.

My thoughts drifted to everything that happened since waking up—stumbling in darkness, wandering through empty streets, hunting for a rickshaw, ending up with a ladyboy bent on encouraging me. And it crossed my mind that none of it was random—from the opening of my eyes to Siriporn's words.

There's a Bible verse I always liked because in the face of hopelessness, it declares hope: "*And we know that in all things God works for the good of those who love him*" (Romans 8:28). Perhaps for the first time, I understood the meaning of those words. They don't promise all will go perfectly—I learned that years ago. What they do promise is God will use everything, including the tragedies and traumas outside his plan, for a greater purpose.

The idea sent shivers up my spine because it wasn't telling me to ignore my past or deny its effect on my life. For years that's what I tried to do—hide, forget, erase, run away. Instead, it says to embrace my suffering. Why? Because God will use it for a greater purpose. It reminds me of another verse that says, "*My grace is sufficient for you, for my power is made perfect in weakness*" (2 Corinthians 12:9). It's another jarring promise that through my brokenness, God will display his strength.

I liked that idea. It meant God wasn't scared of my past. He wasn't dodging my questions or afraid of my doubts. In fact, he was right there through it all, grieving and hurting and crying along with me. Yet he didn't stop there. He refused to give up—no matter the pain I suffered or distance I ran away from him. Even the times I felt light-years removed from his presence, he was drawing me back—loving me, encouraging me, pushing me forward toward redemption. Because that's God's work, meeting me in my most tender, painful place, the spot I've been most deeply wounded, and then doing something miraculous.

If there was ever a time I felt broken and unlovable, it was in this very moment. Yet that's precisely when I grasped God's promise to redeem my past. Not by erasing, or denying, or hiding, but by creating something beautiful and powerful.

The flick of a turn signal shifted my focus from the sky onto Siriporn. She rotated the steering wheel to exit the highway onto a two-lane road. One-story buildings bordered the street and a motor rickshaw passed in the opposite direction. A block away, I saw a blue and white bus parked on the side of the road. We crossed through an intersection and pulled beside it.

Siriporn looked at me with a big smile. "See. I told you."

"Thank you so much," I said, extending my hand. "You have no idea how much you've done for me."

Siriporn laughed. Then she opened her arms, leaned forward, and gave me a hug. Without hesitation, I hugged back. After letting go, I opened the passenger door and stepped outside. With my backpack over my right shoulder, I crossed in front of the Jeep.

"Enjoy your adventure," Siriporn shouted, waving out the window.

I smiled and waved back. "I will."

Siriporn pulled a U-turn and took off down the street toward the highway. Continuing to the bus, I noticed two older women looking at me from inside. With scowling faces, they pointed at me while shaking their heads. I knew they were judging me for getting out of a ladyboy's car after exchanging a hug. They probably assumed I slept with her.

As I walked around the front of the bus and climbed the steps, I couldn't keep myself from chuckling. Because I knew the truth: God used a ladyboy to rescue me.

PART THREE
INDIA

11

WELCOME TO INDIA

A banner announcing my arrival hung between two trees in front of a three-story concrete home. Two dozen children stood in two rows across from one another, from shortest to tallest, boys on the right, girls on the left. The boys sported khaki pants and light blue collared shirts, and the girls wore navy skirts and white ruffled shirts. Each held a pile of flower petals.

The scene reminded me of the sort of makeshift celebrations I saw while working at the White House. Any time a beloved foreign leader visited, a crowd of observers stood outside the black gates with signs and flowers, hoping to catch a glimpse.

Of course, I didn't deserve a celebration. Or even a sign, for that matter. But still, it felt nice to know they looked forward to my arrival.

My nineteen-year-old host, James, parked the SUV and shut off the engine. A boy darted out of line, swung open my door, and circled to the back of the vehicle. Carrying my grey backpack like a baby, he hobbled back in line.

James glanced behind the front seat and smiled. "You may go now, Mr. Paul. The orphans are excited to welcome you." I'd quickly grown to like James, the son of the woman overseeing the orphanage. He grew up assisting his family as they cared for hundreds of children. Now he studied engineering in college. He seemed like an old, wise man in the body of a teenager.

"Alright," I said. "So…I just walk between them or what?"

James chuckled. "Yes, Mr. Paul."

Stiff from the twelve-hour drive, I climbed out of the SUV, set my feet on the dusty road, and stretched my arms above my head. Then I began walking toward the kids. Although I was eager to meet them, I felt uncomfortable with the pomp and circumstance. I didn't want them to see me as special or different.

After all, I traveled to India to make a difference in the lives of children in need. Over the next week I planned to listen to their hopes and dreams, counsel them through pain and trauma, and offer words to lift their spirits.

As I passed between the children, each of them tossed flower petals at me. I laughed as red, purple, and yellow petals landed in my hair and stuck to my clothes. Standing at the end of the line, a middle-aged woman wearing a purple sari that hallmarked her round belly smiled proudly.

When I reached her, she squeezed me with a mannequin hug. I'd heard acts of physical affection between the sexes are frowned upon in India. You seldom even see a couple holding hands. So I accepted the warmth behind her stiffness.

"My name is Kumari," she said with a deep Indian accent. "We welcome you to our home." She took two flower garlands from a child standing beside her and placed them around my neck.

"Thank you," I said, self-conscious about wearing flower necklaces that dangled to my knees.

Kumari bowed and signaled for me to turn around. "Please, watch the children."

I turned and saw the kids facing me in a single line from tallest to shortest. Then on cue, they began singing in perfect harmony. Their voices reminded me of a falsetto choir. The part of their song I understood welcomed me to India and offered a prayer that God would shower me with his blessing and love.

After the song ended, I said, "Thank you. That was beautiful."

The girls hid their faces in modesty while the boys dropped their eyes. I felt like doing the same.

"Would you like to speak to them, Mr. Paul?" James whispered into my ear.

"Of course."

James quickly spoke and the children scrambled into a line in front of me. The first child, a young teenage boy with short black hair and brown eyes, stared at my shoes, occasionally glancing up at my hair then back down. I extended my hand and, after a few seconds, he offered a limp handshake.

"What's your name?" I asked.

James translated my words and the boy whispered a response. A moment later, James announced, "My name is Aadi."

"How are you doing, Aadi?"

Again, James translated and the boy responded in a voice just louder than a breath. "I am great."

I thought for a moment about my next question. "Are you happy here at the orphanage?"

After translating my question and the child's response, James said, "Yes, I am happy."

"Wonderful," I said, just a little taken aback. "What would you like to do when you grow up?"

James translated my question and Aadi's answer. "I would like to be an engineer."

"Okay." I glanced at James and said, "He's ambitious."

"Yes, Mr. Paul. We support the children in their schooling even after they have left our home. We encourage each child to set their sights as high as possible."

"Wow," I said. "That's pretty amazing."

James smiled proudly. "Thank you, Mr. Paul. You are very kind."

I glanced at the child standing behind Aadi. He too looked nervous. Sweat dripped down his forehead and he quickly turned away when he saw me look at him. Then I looked at Aadi again. "Do you have any questions for me?"

James translated and Aadi shook his head. "No, Mr. Paul," James said. "He does not have any questions for you."

"Great." I tried to think of another question but couldn't. The truth is, I didn't expect such an impressive performance. Not that I hoped the kids were troubled or anything. It just didn't seem like they needed anything from me. "Let's move on to the next child."

And so it went for the next hour as I met each child. All of their answers were nearly identical. They were all doing well, they were all happy at the orphanage, they all wanted to be an engineer or pastor or doctor or nurse or teacher (no aspiring lawyers), and none asked a single question. By the end of it, I felt hopeless about getting to know them. They were too afraid of me. Too timid to look me in the eyes. Too nervous to answer my questions with more than single-word responses.

Perhaps they'd never before interacted with a westerner my age or someone of my apparent caste. Or maybe they thought it odd how strikingly similar I looked to the version of Jesus painted on the orphanage walls—white with long dark hair. Or maybe the whole celebration made them think I was a rock star.

Whatever the reason, it left me wondering why I traveled across India to meet these kids. They clearly didn't need my help like I hoped. What, then, was I supposed to do over the next week?

I HAD ARRIVED IN HYDERABAD, INDIA, AT MIDNIGHT TWO DAYS EARlier. Even at midnight, India was chaos. Especially on the roads, where cars and motorbikes and trucks and buses compete for space with cows and dogs and vegetable carts and hordes of people. When Hunny and Jesse—a young couple I met through my oldest brother, Ryan—offered to pick me up on a motor scooter, I politely declined. The three of us riding on an Indian highway seemed a sure way to get myself killed. Instead, we planned to meet in town, where Hunny and I would take a rickshaw while Jesse followed us on his motor scooter.

At the airport, I boarded a shuttle and sat beside a young professional Indian. As we made our way onto the freeway, I asked if I could borrow his cell phone.

He handed me his phone and I dialed Hunny's number. Three rings later she answered. After exchanging hellos, she began firing out instructions. Her heavy accent combined with traffic noise made it impossible for me to understand. So I asked the man beside me if he could find out where I needed to get off the bus.

He took the phone and briefly spoke with Hunny. Then he returned the phone to his pocket. "You must get off now."

"Wait, now? I don't understand. Hunny told you that?"

"Yes. Hurry."

The man raced to the front of the bus and slammed his palm against the plastic partition separating the driver from the passengers. The bus pulled to the side of the road and stopped. Traffic raced past us with blaring horns. I glanced out the window. It was pitch dark and we were in the middle of nowhere. What could I do, though? I picked up my backpack and made my way to the front.

"Where am I supposed to go?" I asked.

The man pointed down the road. "Do you see that bridge?"

I nodded. "Yeah, I think so."

"Walk past it two-hundred meters and you will see a tourist center. That is where your friend will meet you."

"A tourist center? What is that, a building?"

"Yes, it is a building. Now go."

The driver banged a fist on the plastic partition and gestured for me to get off the bus. I stood there a moment as everyone glared at me. I didn't know what to do. Getting off the bus didn't make sense. But I also didn't want to get stuck circling Hyderabad with Hunny and Jesse chasing after me.

"Alright," I finally said.

I walked down the steps and out the door into the evening darkness. It felt like a sauna outside and I wondered if I'd made a mistake. If it wasn't the right location, I didn't know what I'd do. Maybe sleep on the side of the road.

The bus quickly pulled away and merged into a river of traffic. I followed the man's directions and walked along the side of the road over the bridge and toward a light in the distance. Rickshaws, trucks, cars, and buses flew past me with beeping horns. It felt unsafe, even crazy. In an instant, a vehicle could veer a few inches from the road and slam into me.

After half a mile, I reached the light and discovered it wasn't a tourist center. It was a streetlamp. Standing on the side of the highway with traffic roaring past me, I nearly panicked. There was nothing around except racing lights and darkness. I had no way to contact Hunny and Jesse, or anyone else for that matter. I was alone and didn't know what do.

Then I remembered passing a hotel right before the bus stopped. Immediately I turned around and ran—careful not to let my backpack knock me off balance and into the line of vehicles. At a turnoff for the hotel, I slowed to a walk and proceeded down a dirt driveway. I reached a gate and a security guard with a rifle strapped around his back greeted me.

"Guest?" the man asked, staring at me amused. He had a thick mustache above his lip and wore a military-style beret over fluffy black hair.

"No," I said. Then I tried to explain my situation, but it was useless because he didn't know English. I lifted a hand to my ear and mimed talking into a phone. "Telephone?"

A smile broke the man's look of bewilderment, and he bobbled his head—a sign of friendliness in India. Then he removed a phone from his pocket and handed it to me.

Relieved, I called Hunny and told her where to find me. Five minutes later, she and Jesse pulled into the driveway on a motor scooter. I ran over and threw my arms around them.

"Didn't that guy on the bus tell you where to go?" Hunny asked.

"Yeah. He told me to keep walking until I came to the tourist center."

Hunny laughed. "Uh, no. The tourist center is ten kilometers further. You would have been walking all night."

After a full night's rest, Hunny and Jesse showed me around the city. Everything about it captured my attention. Children drifted through the congested city, clinging to a baby brother or sister, riding a bicycle next to speeding traffic, or peddling trinkets. Buffalos, cows, chickens, roosters, dogs, and cats roamed between traffic and on sidewalks. Clothes hung from balconies, windows, and doorways, the colors and fabrics adding to the atmospheric noise. Every building looked faded with age, crumbling apart and imposing a sense of ancient history. Streams of bicycles rode in every direction, rapidly weaving through people and traffic. Old folks weren't hidden away in retirement homes, but sat on doorsteps, manned booths, corralled kids, shooed chickens. Piles of leaves, dried cow pies, and debris smoldered on roadsides, filling the air with smoke that seeped into everything. And everyone—everyone—watched me with fascination.

It seemed like wherever I turned, I saw, smelled, and heard things I would never see, smell, or hear in my normal, everyday life. There was something energizing about it. Immersing myself in a foreign place, a world so different than my own, somehow freed me—perhaps by opening my eyes to every detail.

The next morning, I loaded into James's SUV to begin the twelve-hour road trip to the orphanage in southeastern India. Drifting in and out of sleep, I jolted awake every time James tapped the brakes or slammed the horn to avoid a collision. Once we stopped for a herd of water buffalo crossing the highway. Then we avoided a blind shepherd leading a tribe of goats along the side of the road. Then we wove through motorcycles packed with as many as eight passengers, bicycles drifting across the road, pedestrians walking in the center of traffic, cars swerving across lanes, and monstrous trucks with "Road King" painted on their bumpers.

Halfway through the drive, I began to experience awful cramping. My stomach twisted into a thousand knots, slowly loosened, then constricted again. Reclining in the backseat, I held both hands over my belly and moaned as sweat coated my forehead and my skin turned cold.

"Mr. Paul, are you okay?" James asked. He looked behind the front seat. "What is wrong?" he said, raising his voice. "Are you ill?"

"Yes," I murmured. "Please stop at the next exit. I need to use a restroom."

"Okay, Mr. Paul."

Twenty minutes later, we were still cruising along the highway with no indication of stopping anytime soon.

"Please, James," I finally said, straining my voice. "Find a bathroom. Now."

"But Mr. Paul, there are no sitting toilets nearby. I would like you to relieve yourself in comfort."

"I don't care. This is an emergency."

"Yes, Mr. Paul."

James swerved the SUV to the side of the road, beside three rickety wooden outhouses. I swung the door open and booked it to the first outhouse. Five minutes later I stepped outside.

"Do you feel better, Mr. Paul?" James asked.

I raised a thumb. "Like a different person."

As the evening arrived, we reached the orphanage. And though we somehow escaped an accident along the way, I felt shell-shocked. But it would soon be worth it.

AFTER MY ANTICLIMACTIC INTERVIEWS WITH THE ORPHANS, JAMES escorted me to a remote wing of the orphanage and showed me to my room. I was shocked to see it equipped with an air-conditioning unit, heated shower, and sit-down toilet—luxuries I had acclimated to living without. I left my bag in the room and followed James to private dining quarters, where I sat beside Kumari at the end of a six-foot wooden table. She quickly stood and towered over me. "Please remove," she said, pointing to my pants. She had a smile plastered on her face and spoke forcefully.

"What?" I said. She couldn't possibly mean what I heard her say. Indians are incredibly modest. Commanding me to remove my pants was the last thing I expected.

"Remove," she repeated. Her face grew irritated as she looked down at me.

I shifted my eyes onto James and shook my head like I didn't understand.

"Mr. Paul, she would like you to disrobe so she may wash your trousers."

"Oh," I said loudly, followed by an embarrassed laugh. "Of course."

I scurried to my bedroom, changed into a pair of shorts, and returned with an armful of dirty laundry, clothes I'd worn for days—maybe weeks—without washing. Kumari took my clothes, and she and James left the dining room.

Before long, an elderly woman with grey hair and a white apron entered through swinging doors. She carried two plates with silver covers. After setting the plates in front of me, she lifted the covers, revealing a pile of rice and a roasted chicken. Steam rose from the food and my mouth salivated.

"Is this for me?" I asked.

The woman looked at me confused. I realized she probably didn't know English and felt embarrassed.

"Thank you," I said.

Without speaking, the woman left through the swinging doors. The food looked delicious, but I couldn't believe they prepared it especially for me. I would have been fine eating naan and dal. I didn't have a chance to lift the fork to my mouth, though, because the cook returned carrying another plate and repeated the same routine as before—only this time she uncovered French fries. Then she paraded out a fried bread dish. Then a dozen sauces. Then bread and strawberry jelly. Then sliced mangos. Then bananas. Then sliced papayas. Then a cake with red icing spelling, *Welcome to India Mr. Paul.* Then chocolate and vanilla ice cream. Then a bottle of water. Then a Coke. Then warm buffalo milk and corn flakes.

Looking at the feast, I laughed. Yet I also felt guilty because I couldn't eat more than a bite from each dish. But I tried, stuffing as much food into my mouth as possible—more than I'd eaten since beginning my travels. By the time my stomach felt like it was going to pop, the food still looked untouched.

Eventually I stood from the table, walked down a long hallway, and found James, Kumari, and the rest of their family sitting around a television. Surprised to see me, Kumari stood up, two little girls hid behind a blanket, and an elderly woman stared at me with curiosity.

"How was dinner, Mr. Paul?" James asked.

"Great. Thanks a lot. But I couldn't eat all of it. So I'm sorry about that."

"That's okay," James said, bobbling his head. "We will eat the rest of it."

"Oh." I wondered why they served me warm food while they ate leftovers. I would have preferred to eat with them.

An inquisitive look grew on James's face. "Is there anything else I can do for you, Mr. Paul?"

I shrugged. "I don't think so. What's going on tonight?"

"Whatever you would like."

"Okay," I said slowly. "Well, when do things get started in the morning?"

"Whenever you wake up, Mr. Paul."

"Oh," I said quietly, beginning to pick up on a pattern. "And how about the rest of the week, what's the plan?"

"Every day we will take you to another orphanage unless, of course, you need to rest."

I sighed. "Okay."

"Is everything okay, Mr. Paul?"

Leaning against the door, I considered whether to express my feelings. While I didn't want to sound ungrateful, I also didn't want them to expect too much from me. And based on my earlier interaction with the orphans, it didn't seem like I would have much to offer. "Actually, I'm not really sure what good it'll do."

James tilted his head. "What do you mean, Mr. Paul?"

"Well, it just didn't seem like I had much luck connecting with the kids. What I mean is, it might be hard for me to help much." I paused a moment to gather my thoughts. "Which is fine. I just don't want anyone to think I'm a superhero or something."

James laughed. "No, Mr. Paul. No one thinks you are a superhero. The children just want to show you God's love."

"Oh." I nodded my head slowly, letting the words sink in deep. "They want to show *me* God's love."

James bobbled his head again. "Yes, so please, Mr. Paul, get some rest. We will leave once you wake. Otherwise, it will get too hot for you."

After thanking James again for dinner, I made my way to my room. Looking out a window onto a courtyard below, I watched some children kick a soccer ball back and forth. To be honest, I wanted to be a superhero to those kids. I wanted to parachute into their lives, offer some wisdom and encouragement, maybe even say a prayer. But as I was learning, they didn't really need me or my help. In fact, they undoubtedly had more to offer than I had to give.

Why, then, were James and his family treating me like royalty? I didn't want my clothes washed. I didn't want air conditioning or a sit-down toilet or a warm shower. I didn't want big meals prepared for me. I didn't want anyone to wait on me. I didn't want so much for free—it was embarrassing because they couldn't really afford it and I didn't deserve it. I had nothing to offer, nothing to give, nothing to provide in return.

As I continued watching the kids race around the makeshift soccer field—bricks serving as goals, the ball flat, wearing tattered sandals—I wondered if the problem wasn't with my inability to help, but instead my inability to receive love. After all, that's what they were doing—loving me. And that meant honoring and serving and providing.

Perhaps that's why God brought me across the globe to a tiny orphanage in southeastern India. To teach me how to accept love without condition, without warrant, without merit, and without justification.

12

PREACHING TO MYSELF

Sweat beaded on my forehead the moment I stepped out of the car and into the heat. Motes of dust reflected light from the noonday sun and the scent of manure hung heavy in the air. I extended a hand toward an Indian man wearing dirt-stained pants and a sweat-soiled button-down shirt. He nervously smiled, wrapped his clammy hands around my hand, and spoke in muddled words.

On the other side of the car, James slammed the door, then raced to my side. "He says he is honored to meet you."

"I'm honored to meet you, as well."

As James translated my words, the man smiled and looked down.

"It's really hot," I whispered, glancing at James while brushing a hand through my already-damp hair. "Can we get out of the sun?"

"Yes, Mr. Paul. Let me ask."

James uttered a few words, and the man grabbed my arm and whisked me down a dirt pathway. As we headed toward a shack, we passed an old church. In its heyday, I'm sure it looked beautiful and imbued its parishioners with pride. Now it was an eyesore. Cracks and missing pieces scarred the stained-glass windows, and off-white paint peeled from the few wood panels that remained. At the doorway, a crowd of men and women overflowed outside. Someone must have noticed us because suddenly everyone's eyes shifted onto me. I lifted a hand and some people waved back.

At the shack, the man swung open the door and we walked inside. The only light came from a shaded window and the air smelled dank. The man directed me to a bamboo chair. I sat down while he grabbed a fan from a corner. He dropped it on a coffee table and turned it to its highest setting. Then he raced into another room, leaving James and me alone.

With the fan blowing on my face, I glanced at James and grinned. Over the past week, we'd spent a lot of time together visiting his family's sister orphanages throughout southeastern India. I made a point of showing interest in each child, receiving their love, and speaking affirmation into their lives. Sometimes I took photos and displayed the results on my camera screen— something that always elicited giggles. Other times I prayed for their health, families, and futures. Mostly, though, I just spent time with them, talking and laughing and playing games. There was nothing better than seeing their smiles.

Between orphanages, James showed me around. My favorite stops were always the slums—pockets of poverty in already-impoverished communities. With a camera in hand, I roamed down narrow alleyways and between makeshift homes pieced together with tarps and branches, James always trailing close behind. Kids surrounded me wherever I went, competing for my attention and trying to get me to take their photo. Adults stood back and watched, bewildered by my presence.

One time while photographing a group of boys and girls, a few teenagers approached us gripping wood boards. These guys looked different than the others—suspicious, maybe angry. James stepped in front of them, blocking their path, and spoke in a firm voice. They puffed their chests.

"Mr. Paul," James said. "We must leave now."

"Why?" I looked at the teenagers and saw them glaring at James and me.

James whispered into my ear. "They will beat us up if we do not go."

"So what?" I turned back toward the children and snapped another photo.

James grabbed my shoulder. "Mr. Paul. We *must* go. Now." He put his hand on my back and pushed me forward.

"Fine." I waved goodbye to the kids, then quickly followed James through a maze of alleys. By the time we reached the SUV, I realized how stupid I'd been back there. James had a right to be afraid. Who knows what would've happened if he hadn't been there?

This, however, was our last journey together. In the morning I flew to Bangalore, then for the next two weeks I worked my way through southern India and, during my final week, traveled with Alissa. But first, I needed to get through today.

The man returned carrying two orange juice boxes and a plastic tray of cookies. He set them on the table and with an open hand signaled for me to partake. I quickly downed an orange juice and grabbed a cookie. Across the room, the man sat on a couch and studied me intently.

"Thank you," I said between bites.

James translated and the man blushed, then flashed a big smile. Tapping my foot on the floor, I anxiously looked around the room and tried to think of something to say. Then I realized James had yet to eat or drink anything. So I handed him the other box of orange juice.

"No, Mr. Paul," he said, pushing the box away. "It is for you."

"Are you sure? You're not thirsty?"

"No, Mr. Paul. I am not thirsty. And you must refresh yourself."

I returned the juice to the table and took another cookie. After biting it in half, I glanced at James again. "Do you know how many people are at the church?"

James translated my question and the man responded. With every word, his voice grew more enthusiastic and his hands reached higher into the air. Lowering his voice, he brought his hands close together.

"There are one hundred people there," James finally said. "Half are pastors from surrounding villages. The other half are widows who have no home or family, and many of them are very ill."

"And," I said quietly as butterfly wings flapped in my stomach, "they're all waiting for me." Shaking my head slowly, I placed the rest of the cookie into my mouth and began chewing.

"Yes, Mr. Paul. They are all waiting for you. Are you ready now?"

I thought about James's question. "Not quite."

WHEN JAMES ASKED IF I WANTED TO SPEAK AT A CHURCH SERVICE, I told him no. It's one thing to give my testimony at a youth event like I did in Indonesia a couple months earlier. It's something entirely different to prepare and give a sermon to a roomful of adults at a church.

Growing up, I never felt comfortable being a Christian. Perhaps it was because I lived in Oregon, where most people aren't believers. Automatically that made me different. I learned that lesson on my first day of kindergarten. Everyone sat in a circle and, one by one, shared what their dad did for a living. When my turn came, I proudly declared, "My dad's a pastor."

The room went silent.

After that, I never again wanted to talk about religion in public. I didn't want to mention my dad's job or that I went to church every Sunday. It made me uncomfortable because I sensed other people felt uncomfortable.

As I grew older, though, I began feeling guilty about my silence. Christians are supposed to speak up and defend truth, evangelize and share the gospel, push against immorality and sin—at least that's what I thought. That guilt motivated me to begin speaking more about my faith. But I still didn't enjoy it.

Then one summer in high school, I attended a two-week conference in the mountains of Colorado. For ten hours a day, we listened to lecture after lecture about topics relating to our faith. We learned about the Bible, apologetics, comparative religions, cultural issues, politics, and science. Not necessarily for the purpose of strengthening our faith, but to equip ourselves to debate.

One afternoon, we went to a park and argued about abstract topics like the morality of vehicular speeding. Another afternoon, we picketed against a business we weren't supposed to like. One morning, we went into town and tried to convert unsuspecting folks at a laundromat.

On my way home from Colorado, I determined to ignore my feelings of discomfort and put my newfound evangelism into action. It didn't take long. As the plane landed in Portland, I launched into a heated debate with an atheist sitting behind me. The following month when school started, fear no longer held me back. The discomfort and awkwardness I previously felt wilted beside my faith-filled fire.

In no time I developed a reputation as someone who loved arguing about religion and politics. Whether debating friends or classmates or even teachers, I never backed down from a fight. I knew the truth and it was my job to proclaim it.

Deep down, though, I hated every minute of it. I hated arguing. I hated disagreement. I hated offending people. I hated creating waves. I hated the gathering discomfort around me. And paradoxically, the more I argued the less secure I felt about my faith. It seemed as though encountering someone with opinions even slightly different than my own surfaced the possibility I might be wrong. It was as if the existence of divergence cast a shadow upon my own views. Over time I suspect I elevated rightness above truth.

Eventually, the conflict wore me out. Halfway through my sophomore year of college, I found myself verging on apathy. Although I still valued my faith, I didn't want to talk about it. I just wanted to live without conflict. In a sense, I reverted to the same passive tendencies I had as a child. I started avoiding debates. I began sidestepping deep conversations. I no longer shared my opinions eagerly. During philosophical discussions with friends or classmates, I opted to observe rather than participate. Not completely, just more often.

Years later, during my cross-country move back to Oregon, I stayed overnight with a friend in California named Jono. We'd been roommates in DC for a while and knew each other well. I enjoyed hanging out with him because he was so different than me—fiery and spontaneous. That night, we went to an outdoor shopping area in Santa Monica to eat dinner and walk around. At one point, Jono spotted some Orthodox Jews and approached them. He wasn't confrontational or anything; he simply had a question and asked it.

Over the next ten minutes, Jono shared a deeper and more enlightening spiritual conversation with people he had never met than I had shared with anyone in years. It was humbling. And it helped me realize how far astray I had wandered. Not because I had never randomly approached a group of Orthodox Jews. But because I had disengaged from my deeply-held beliefs. I had essentially hidden what little light I carried under a cardboard box.

That experience reinforced something I had begun realizing about myself. I'm not a fighter. That might seem trivial, but I struggled against it for much of my life. For years I tried to force myself to act a certain way and it just didn't fit. I thought to be a Christian meant to be confrontational and argumentative. But that wasn't me.

At my core, I crave peace. Where there's division, I want reconciliation. Where there's unrest, I seek stability. Where there's disagreement, I look for common ground. Where there's offense, I strive for forgiveness. That's who I am. There's no sense fighting it. In all things, I wanted to strive for respect and understanding. Those are the values I wanted to embody. That's how I felt comfortable expressing my faith.

Here's the thing, though. Timidity and indifference still pulled on me. Sometimes I avoided expressing myself when I wanted to say something. Sometimes I didn't raise my voice when it would have been appropriate. Sometimes I remained silent when I needed to speak.

That's what happened when I told James I wouldn't preach. I gave in to my deepest fears—the voice telling me it's easier, and therefore better, to remain silent than to speak truth.

By the next morning, though, I changed my mind and told James I would do it. Fear wouldn't stop me. Not this time. For years it held me back and kept me from being myself. But not anymore. I had to put into practice what I had long suspected: Fear is never a good excuse for inaction. It's always a distraction, always a diversion.

ONCE I WORKED MY WAY THROUGH ALL THE COOKIES, I ROSE FROM the bamboo chair. The man on the couch jumped to his feet. He looked excited, and I sensed it rubbing off on me.

"Are you ready, Mr. Paul?" James asked.

I nodded. "Yup. Let's do this thing."

The man rushed in front of us, opened the front door, and led us up the pathway to the old church. Walking toward the building, my heart pounded. Then I stepped through the doorway. Each pew was packed. Every eye followed me as I proceeded down the center aisle. I stepped onto the stage and stood behind the podium.

As James introduced me, I noticed two water stains gathering on the floor beside me. Then I realized it wasn't water but sweat dripping from my hair. It was hot—very hot. Even with the front door propped open, the air inside remained stagnant. I looked out over the crowd. Women, gaunt with shriveled skin, filled the back half of the church. Men drenched in sweat and with bloodshot eyes occupied the front half.

Everyone watched me. No one made a sound.

FOR A TIME IN MY EARLY TWENTIES, I SENSED I STOOD ON THE EDGE of a spiritual epiphany—an insight I hoped would revolutionize how I viewed and interacted with God. It would transform what had become a structured, rote belief-system into a radical, fresh faith.

I wanted God to impact the world...my world. I wanted prayer to cause miracles. I wanted faith to move mountains. I wanted what I believed to alter how I engaged with others. I knew it was only a matter of time before I received this life-changing revelation. Occasionally I heard a sermon that moved me or noticed something striking while reading the Bible, and wondered if that was it. But within days, the insight faded, leaving me the same as before.

Every time, I returned to waiting—certain God would one day "show up" in a dramatic way. Then I heard a preacher talk about incorporating faith into every part of your life. You shouldn't consider a certain time of the day or week holy, he said, because all time is equally holy. A light bulb went off in my mind—by setting aside specific time to pray and read the Bible, I had unknowingly cabined God in my life. I only allowed his presence during those specific moments. So I abandoned my daily time with God, convinced it would somehow revitalize my faith. But this only pushed me further from God.

Eventually, I grew tired of waiting for a revelation from God, figuring the conviction must have been a reflection of my own desire to connect with the divine on a more personal level. God hadn't intended to speak to me, I concluded. Because if he had, I would have noticed.

All these years later, I'm no longer convinced God didn't "show up" in my life. What I mean is, what if God has always been present in my life, only I've overlooked him? Perhaps by expecting a booming-voice-from-the-sky revelation, I've ignored the quiet voice of God whispering to me every day.

What if God most often communicates, not through dramatic encounters, but through ordinary, everyday life—through his "still small voice?" That's not to say he can't appear as fire in a bush, or rain down loaves of bread, or split open the sea, or speak through a donkey. Maybe, though, God chooses to work in softer, subtler ways.

The slow transformation of our heart through prayer and obedience. The refreshing of our mind through daily reading of the Scripture. The encouraging word from a friend when we're weighed down by pain. The sunset in the sky when we're feeling unloved. The smile of a stranger when we're feeling unnoticed. The phone call from a parent or sibling at just the right time. The unseen opportunity we couldn't have anticipated. The list could go on…and it surely does in each of our lives.

The only reason I didn't see God, I think, is because I had my eyes fixed on the sky when I should have been looking directly in front of me. It's the same reason, I believe, we too often fail to see

God today—because our expectations limit our sight. Perhaps when we lower our eyes, we'll see God staring back at us.

It's not climactic. It's not dramatic. It's not necessarily even exciting. But it's real. And ironically, by seeing God in the little things, I suspect we'll find deeper meaning in our daily lives. Because finally we'll glimpse not only how much God loves us, but how he's using us to love others.

ONCE I FINISHED SPEAKING, I BRUSHED MY HAND THROUGH MY SWEAT-drenched hair. I looked down and saw two puddles on the floor beside me. James quickly grabbed my hand and pulled me off the stage.

"We must leave, Mr. Paul," he said. "Your body is overheating."

He led me down the aisle, past outstretched hands and a collision of incomprehensible words. I reached back, trying to touch everyone's hands, but James continued dragging me forward. Toward the back of the church, women poured into the aisle, clutching my arms and clothes. Their faces, creased and saggy, looked full of sadness and sorrow. My heart ached as James tugged me between their delicate bodies.

As we stepped out of the church, James and I nearly stumbled over an old woman sitting on the ground. When she saw us, she extended her hands into the air and opened her mouth. Slurred words tumbled out. She looked sick and I thought I saw a tear roll down her cheek. Without thinking, I knelt beside her. Then I saw something I'll never forget—sunken skin where I should have seen eyes.

In that moment, a flood of doubts crashed over me. I couldn't do anything for this woman—or any of these people. She needed a doctor, not some wannabe preacher. Maybe I could pray, but that would be awkward. And probably ineffective.

A few seconds later, James pulled me up and we continued to the air-conditioned car. As we drove back to the orphanage, I struggled to make sense of everything. Then I asked James if he remembered the blind woman.

"Yes, Mr. Paul. I remember her. Why do you ask?"

"I don't know," I said, shaking my head. "I just wish there was something I could've done. Could you make out what she was saying?"

"Yes. She said 'Thank you for your beautiful message.' And then she asked God to give you a wife."

"Wait, I don't understand. She said what?"

"They are used to hearing lengthy sermons. Two hours, even. She was relieved by your brevity."

"And the thing about a wife?"

"Yes. Most Indian men at your age are married. She probably felt worried for you."

"Oh. Why was she outside then? It looked like she'd fallen or something."

James laughed. "No, Mr. Paul. She sat outside to stay cool because the church was warm. She is very clever indeed."

"So you're telling me she didn't ask me to pray for her? She didn't ask me to heal her?"

James laughed again. "No, Mr. Paul. She did not ask you to heal her. She is a very happy woman and the church takes good care of her. She only wanted to thank you and pray for you. But

I'm sure she would have been very honored by your prayer. It would have made her the talk of the village."

Still, for the rest of the drive, I thought about the blind woman and how, in that situation and so many others, I felt blind too—oblivious to God's greater plans and purposes. It used to frustrate me, not knowing my future. I'd spend hours and days plotting and planning the trajectory of my life, and then a new, unseen opportunity would appear—or a door I hoped might open slammed shut—and my life would shift in an entirely new direction.

All the worrying, all the strategizing, all the scheming was futile. Yet like an impulse I continued doing it. But now, I was beginning to accept—no, embrace—my limitations. I really could trust God with my future, as unnerving as that sometimes seemed. The past two and a half months proved it. In fact, my entire life proved it.

Which made me wonder who I'd really been preaching to back at the church. Because of all people, I was the one who needed a reminder that God's at work in each and every moment.

Even when I don't know it or can't feel it.

13

WANDERING
THROUGH KERALA

The public bus snaked up the narrow road, inches from plunging off the edge of a mountain. A cool breeze blew through the open windows, bringing with it the musky scent of tea leaves and burning spices. A crowd of Indians napped around me, young and old alike. Shifting my eyes from one side of the bus to the other, I watched the scenery, transfixed by the unfolding beauty. Every bend of the road revealed a thousand new sights.

Brown and grey rust blended together on scrap metal fences. Mossy stone steps zigzagged up hills blanketed in vegetation. Water trickled down rock walls, etching vein-like paths into granite. Concrete homes perched from the side of an almost-vertical hill, each door red, green, purple, or blue. Elephants trudged up a road, dragging worn chains behind them.

Green-tea bushes stretched across a sea of rolling hills, perfectly symmetrical trails tracing the contours of the landscape. Beyond the hills, a distant mountain, dense with trees, reached into the sky. Two waterfalls wound down the mountain, plumes of mist bursting upward at each twist. Wispy clouds capped the mountain's jagged peak, and against the bright horizon, skeletal branches wove an intricate lace design. Above the fog, the sky exploded with a yellow glow. Scattered throughout the valley, hundreds of small white crosses rose from the tops of stone cathedrals.

Yet in the midst of such overwhelming beauty, I felt myself nearing a breakdown.

Hours earlier, Alissa had written a crushing email—she was considering calling off her trip to India. Apparently she started thinking about the logistics of our relationship. After a week together in India, I would return to Oregon and she would travel to Kenya. Two months later, she would fly to DC and I would move to Mississippi—where I had landed a year-long clerkship with a federal judge.

That meant long-distance wasn't a temporary hurdle. It was a continuing reality. To be honest, it scared me too. I hated the idea of not seeing Alissa for weeks at a time, not having her by my side, not sharing life together. Of all people, I knew how that felt. The past three months had torn me apart. I too didn't know if I could make it another year.

But I wanted to try. Until three hours ago, I thought Alissa wanted to as well. Now I doubted it. I didn't know if I could handle losing her. I'd been looking forward to our reunion since the moment I arrived in Indonesia. Every night I dreamed about seeing her. Every day I anticipated embracing her. That's what kept me going through all the loneliness of traveling by myself.

More than that, I was growing convinced we might one day get married. Sure, she was my first serious girlfriend and we hadn't yet said we loved each other. But I truly believed God had a plan for us that went beyond India and long-distance dating. It involved getting married and building a life together; having kids and growing old. Everything I always wanted. Everything I hoped for. With Alissa, I thought I'd found it. Now I didn't know.

In response to her email, I tried to conceal my panic. That's how I felt, though. Panicked. Over the course of an hour I drafted three emails. The first let everything out—all the pain and fear. Then I wrote a version laying out every logical reason for her to fly to India. The last email took neither approach. I simply told her how much I cared for her and wanted to see her. I acknowledged I too didn't know the future, but trusted God had a plan. Otherwise we were both in trouble. I signed off with a prayer—asking God to grant Alissa the wisdom she needed to make the right decision.

That's the email I ended up sending. I deleted the others. Then I hopped on a bus to Munnar, a small town deep in the Western Ghats—a mountain range running parallel to India's western coast.

As I looked out the window onto the most beautiful land-scape I had seen, my emotions cascaded. All the built-up hope and approaching disappointment collided, forming a tidal wave of emotion. A knot dropped in my throat. My eyes misted. The edges of my lips fell. My cheeks began contracting. I glanced round the bus—no one seemed to notice I was teetering on the verge of tears.

Then, suddenly and without warning, the wave receded.

THE MOST VIVID MEMORY OF MY CHILDHOOD IS THE TIME I SAW MY family's cocker spaniel, Misty, sprawled across the backseat of our car with her stomach ripped open. I was five years old.

Earlier in the day, Misty had escaped from our house after someone left the front door open. She sprinted outside and took off down the hill. I attempted to follow but quickly gave up. From our driveway, I shouted her name and tried to entice her with her favorite snack—cheese. It wasn't the first time Misty had run away. Usually, though, she returned.

Eventually, a car stopped in front of our house. A woman stepped out looking flustered. I ran inside and got my mom. As she walked toward the woman, I nervously watched from the doorway. Then the woman grasped my mom's arm and spoke into her ear. My mom's face dropped.

They stepped toward the woman's car, opened the back door, and my mom leaned inside. Then she turned. In her arms, she held Misty—a dog I had known as long as I could remember, a dog I loved as much as anyone in the world. Carrying our beloved family member, she walked by me and placed her in the backseat of our car.

As I stood over Misty, her insides exposed and blood seeping from her stomach, she struggled to stare up at me. Her eyes looked afraid and she panted frantically. I tried to speak, to tell her I loved her, but I couldn't. Then my mom got in the car and started the engine. And I knew if I was going to say something, it was now.

Slowly, I leaned toward Misty and pressed my face against her soft head. Then I wrapped my arms around her furry neck and squeezed tight.

"Why'd you have to run away?" I whispered.

While my mom took Misty to the vet, I stayed home and a neighbor watched me. Against a flood of sadness, I tried to remain strong—holding back tears and hiding my emotion. Then around noon, I did what I did every other weekday. I ran outside, climbed the stairs of a bus, and went to school.

For as long as I can remember, I've had a hard time showing emotion. I suspect it's because vulnerability drew my brothers' ridicule. Every time I dropped my guard, they attacked. It seems natural I would develop a defense mechanism to keep my emotions in check. To my young brain, emotion equaled victimization.

I think that's why I went to school after seeing Misty on the verge of death. By missing class, I would be acknowledging the pain. There would be no concealing it. No denying the sadness. But if I pushed on with my day, I could keep it secret. No one would ever know, and I could avoid the humiliation. At least that was the plan.

That evening, I stood in our backyard and watched Ryan lower a shovel into the ground, crack open the earth, and gather a pile of dirt beside me. Before long, tears began trickling down my face. Then I began sobbing, my tears dripping into the soil.

While I cried, a friend from school stood beside me. Not comforting me. Not consoling me. Not reassuring me. But laughing at me.

This reinforced what I had already learned. Emotions only lead to more pain. So at all costs they are to remain hidden. Suppressed. Buried. That's what led to the creation of the defense mechanism. And sure enough, as time passed it grew more effective. Crying soon became a thing of the past, something I once did but not anymore. It was too risky.

By the time I became an adolescent, I stopped crying altogether. Not even when my grandmother died and I saw her body carted into a hearse. Days later, my family traveled to Ohio for her funeral. After returning, a friend asked where I'd gone.

"My grandmother's funeral," I told her.

She looked at me suspiciously. "You're joking."

"No, I'm not. There's nothing funny about it."

"Then why are you smiling?"

I didn't know how to respond. The truth is, losing my grandmother felt like losing part of my childhood. She'd celebrated every Christmas with my family. During the final years of her life, she moved across the country to be near us. She became a regular presence in my life. It hurt to lose her. But I couldn't show it. All I could do was mask the pain.

It would be another four years until the defense mechanism momentarily failed. And it would take the sudden and unexpected death of someone I loved—Bonnie Witherall. Years earlier her husband, Gary, lived with my family before they got married. After their wedding, they lived nearby and often hung out at our house. We'd eat dinner, then Gary and I would play computer games while Bonnie talked with my parents. Over time, Gary became the kind older brother I'd always wanted. And Bonnie—she became the sister I'd always needed.

Eventually they moved to Lebanon to serve the people there. Then, in the early hours of November 21, Bonnie woke up and walked to the women's clinic where she worked. After turning on the lights, she heard a knock at the door. She opened it like she always did. Instead of a frightened woman seeking help like so many times before, this time it was an unknown man. He pointed a gun at her head and shot three times.

Hours later my dad called to tell me what happened. I couldn't believe it. She was so young and overflowing with life. Only days earlier she wrote an email about walking along the Mediterranean Sea, listening to praise music and feeling an overwhelming sense of joy because she felt God's presence. How could she no longer exist? How could someone take such a loving woman? How could someone snuff out such a bright light?

Within minutes of hearing the news, I forced myself to go to class. I couldn't focus on the professor, though. It all seemed pointless. Halfway through, I snuck out, got in my truck, and drove to my parents' house ninety minutes north. On the way there, I listened to a Third Day mix. As soon as "All the Heavens" started playing, tears flowed down my face.

As your children gather in peace,
All the angels sing in heaven.
In your temple all that I seek,
Is to glimpse your holy presence.
(© Universal Music Publishing Group)

Before I got home, I dried my cheeks and composed myself. Then I saw my dad—and I couldn't hold it in any longer. I fell into his arms and together we sobbed. The same thing happened at her funeral several days later. I tried to remain strong, but I couldn't. The pain was too great. Bonnie had become a martyr for her faith. And that was a holy tragedy.

That was the last time I cried. Not when three girls, one after the other, broke my heart. Not during the loneliest, most depressing and angst-ridden days in DC. Not even when I finally opened up to a friend about what Adam did to me. Not once did I shed a tear. And it was no longer because I didn't want to cry. I simply didn't know how.

As dusk fell, the bus pulled into Munnar. Green hills surrounded the small, quiet town. The cool air offered a welcome relief from the suffocating heat elsewhere in India. I had spent the prior week traveling around the southern portion of the country. From Rajahmundry, I flew to Bangalore and stayed with a friend of a friend from Rwanda. Then I traveled to the congested city of Trivandrum, where I slept in a filthy room infested by termites. The next day, I squeezed into an overcrowded train and headed north to Alappuzha. Then I took a boat to Kottayam and a public bus through the Western Ghats to Kumily, the home of the beautiful Periyar National Park.

Now, stepping off the bus in Munnar, I had a single obsessive thought—Alissa. I made my way to an internet café. It'd been five hours since I emailed her; nine since she emailed me. She was half a day behind, which meant she sent her email before she went to bed. If she woke up early, she may have already read my response. Maybe she'd responded.

At a flickering monitor, I pulled up my email—but I didn't see a new message. Perhaps she didn't want to respond. Maybe because she didn't want to tell me what she'd already decided—that she wouldn't come to India. Or maybe she was still asleep. I hoped.

I left the internet café and found a place to stay overlooking a tea plantation. With my camera in hand, I headed back outside, ate a small dinner from a street vendor, and trekked into the hills. Following pathways etched between rows of tea plants,

I wandered over rolling hills, one after another. Each time I climbed a hill, I rested at its peak, gazing at the valley below.

As I turned onto a narrow pathway, I saw a boy in the distance. Walking up a hill, his head shifted back and forth like he was looking for someone or something. Curious, I caught up.

"Hey," I said from steps behind.

He turned around and smiled. "Hello, mister."

"What are you looking for?"

"Follow me." He turned back around and continued up the hill.

I took a step forward, then hesitated. "Where are you going?"

"You will see," he said, glancing at me over his shoulder.

I stood there a moment, watching the boy walk away. Over the past ten weeks, I'd grown skeptical of advice. It seemed everyone had an agenda, everyone had an angle. When locals saw me, they assumed because I was a foreigner and alone, they could take advantage of me. Out of necessity, I developed a thick skin. This boy seemed different, though. For some reason, I trusted his intentions and decided to follow him.

We walked beside each other down one pathway and up another until we reached a stone stairway. It led up a steep hill covered in green-tea bushes.

"Up there, I think," the boy said, pointing toward the top of the hill.

"What is it?"

He stared up. "You will see."

Carefully, the boy climbed the stairs, using his hands to steady himself on the ground. I took a deep breath, allowing the cool moist air to fill my lungs. Then I followed after him. As I climbed each step, I thought about Alissa's email. The possibility of ending up alone terrified me. That wasn't something I wanted to go through again. In five months I would turn twenty-nine. I had been alone far too long—and I feared entering my thirties without someone by my side. I wanted that person to be her. I wanted my search to be over.

As my emotions built, then just as quickly receded, I heard the soft whimper of a child. It sounded too young to come from the boy. Maybe not, though. Maybe he fell and hurt himself. I picked up my speed to find out.

When I reached the top, I saw the boy standing next to an old temple. The small concrete structure looked rundown, like it had fallen into disrepair after years of neglect. Beside the boy stood a young child—presumably his little brother. Maybe that's who he'd been looking for all this time.

The little boy's head swayed between his shoulders and his face looked flush, like he'd been crying. The older boy wrapped an arm around his shoulder and spoke softly. Although I couldn't understand his words, I sensed he was telling him everything would be alright. He didn't need to worry any longer. He'd been found.

After a minute, the little boy raised his head. Bashfully, he lifted his hand and waved at me. I smiled and waved back. Then the older boy pointed toward the west.

"Look," he said.

I turned around—and finally I saw what he had promised. Green hills stretched across the landscape divided by perfectly symmetrical pathways. Scattered clouds dotted the sky, casting shadows on the lush tea bushes below. Rays of sunshine broke through the gathering fog, bathing everything in gold.

Eventually, the two boys walked past me holding hands. I watched as the older boy helped his younger brother down the stairway to the bottom of the hill. Then they continued along a pathway, disappearing a moment later.

Raising my eyes, I looked out over the valley. I stood there a while, taking in the beauty and letting my mind relax.

After the sun vanished below the horizon, I made my way down the hill and back to my hotel. Before heading inside, I decided to check my email again. Maybe in the hour and a half since I last checked, Alissa had responded. So I walked down the road to the internet café. It was dark by now and the streets were almost empty. An occasional streetlamp created enough light to make my way along the sidewalk.

At the internet café, I sat in front of the same flickering monitor and pulled up my email. That's when I saw a message from Alissa. At first I didn't want to open it. I feared what it might say.

But then I realized, even if she did give up—even if she never spoke to me again—I would be alright. As strange as it may sound, I sensed I'd been found by God over the course of my travels. After years of running from my past and everything I refused to face, getting lost in bad places surrounded by bad people, I finally understood God had been searching for me all along.

Even when I thought all hope was lost, God never stopped looking. He kept searching and searching. And on the other side of the world, he'd found me. Now, I didn't need to worry any longer. I could finally relax. I could lower my guard. Maybe one day I could even cry in his presence.

After a deep breath, I opened Alissa's email.

Paul,

You're right. God does have a plan, and I need to continue trusting that all of this is happening for a reason. God brought us together after I'd already given up, and now isn't the time to throw up my hands and walk away. You're worth the risk. I can't wait to see you in India.

Yours,
Alissa

P.S. Sorry for freaking out. Last night was tough. When I woke up this morning, I felt a renewed sense of hope. Then I read your email. Thank you so much for understanding and responding with grace. That was exactly what I needed. You're exactly what I need. Have fun today—or tomorrow, I guess—exploring India!

After reading the message once, then twice, then three times, I breathed a sigh of relief. Then I sent a quick message back.

Alissa,

You made my day. Thank you!

Paul

I left the internet café and returned to my hotel. For the rest of the night, I couldn't stop smiling. Because in one week, Alissa and I would finally be together.

14

TOGETHER AT LAST

At three o'clock in the morning, a dramatic symphony track blared from overhead speakers at the Hyderabad airport. Every four minutes the track repeated itself. A swarm of men, women, and children impatiently waited with their eyes locked on the doorway. The whooshing of every airplane overhead triggered murmurs throughout the crowd.

I stood in the middle of it all, eagerly waiting for Alissa. While exhausted, I also felt grateful. Only nineteen hours ago, I discovered my flight from Kochi to Hyderabad had been canceled. I called the airline and begged them to put me on another flight. Alissa and I only had six days together. Every minute apart was a minute lost. Plus, I didn't want her arriving in India without me to welcome her. That was the worst-case scenario.

Apparently the begging worked because the agent found me a flight. Unfortunately, it left in two hours and involved a twelve-hour layover in Bangalore. That meant I wouldn't have time to sleep and shower in Hyderabad. It also meant nothing could go wrong. Even a short delay would keep me from welcoming Alissa.

But still, I'd found a way to get to Hyderabad. Ecstatic, I ran through the rain back to my hotel, stuffed everything into my backpack, and caught an auto rickshaw to the airport. When I handed my ticket to an agent, she looked at it and frowned.

"I'm sorry to inform you," she said. "But your flight has been canceled."

I stared at her in disbelief. Somehow I forced out a question. "Is there another flight?"

The woman typed on a keyboard, then smiled. "Yes." Seconds later, she printed a new ticket and handed it to me. To my surprise, I had a direct flight to Hyderabad that arrived five hours before Alissa. I would have time to sleep and shower before her 3:30 a.m. arrival.

Ten hours later, I boarded my flight and traveled to Hyderabad. When I arrived, I took a shuttle to an overnight visitor's center—a brief-stay dorm-style hotel at the airport. Surrounded by a roomful of empty beds, I tossed and turned for the next few hours. At 2:30, I rolled out of bed, cleaned up, and found the concourse for international arrivals.

As I stood among the crowd of anxious Indians, I reflected on how far Alissa and I had come over the past three months. It's said distance makes the heart grow fonder. That was certainly true of me. In the past three months, I had gone from liking her to potentially loving her. It seemed miraculous Alissa felt the same way.

I found myself daydreaming about the next six days. Although I wanted to spend every moment together, I knew that wasn't a good idea. I didn't want to cross any lines and do something we would regret. So that meant sleeping in separate rooms. Other than those six or seven hours, though, we would have plenty of time to explore India, eat delicious food, talk about anything and everything, and enjoy ourselves.

Of course, there was also *the* conversation hanging over my head, the moment we truly opened our hearts and told each other about out pasts. I felt I could handle whatever she planned to say. She dated several guys before me and I suspected it involved one of them. I didn't have as much confidence the other way—not because I'm more gracious or anything. My past is different, though.

Abuse carries such a dark stigma, regardless of the severity or circumstances. This is especially true in some Christian communities. I didn't want her to judge me or consider me less of a man. I didn't want her to question my sexuality or complicity in what happened. Those are natural questions from someone who hasn't suffered abuse, understandable even, but they're also painful.

There are few rules when it comes to abuse, particularly affecting children and adolescents. Everyone is impacted differently, wounded in a uniquely tragic way. All I knew was what I experienced. And though it affected me through the years, and in some ways probably always would, it didn't define me. Jesus, and only Jesus, defined me.

Perhaps that seems too simple. And maybe it is. The last thing I wanted was to shut my eyes to what happened and its lingering reverberations on my life. But after months of counseling and processing, a great deal of healing and restoration, even a bit of anger and confrontation, it's ultimately where I landed. Abuse is part of my past, an element of my story. But it's not everything. God is doing something bigger, redeeming my brokenness and creating something beautiful. That's what I wanted to convey because it's what I believe.

I couldn't wait to get that conversation out of the way—so we could move forward. Maybe that wouldn't be possible. Maybe Alissa couldn't handle my past. I understood the risk. But it was a risk I needed to take. And that meant raising it sooner rather than later.

After an hour of anxious waiting, people began trickling out the door carrying backpacks and pulling suitcases. Standing on my tiptoes and peeking over heads and between bodies, I scoured the doorway, searching for Alissa's face. A group walked out and celebration erupted from somewhere in the crowd. Five minutes later, another group emerged and another explosion of joy broke out. Then another five minutes. Then ten minutes. Then twenty minutes. Then thirty minutes.

And then I saw her.

Nothing could have prepared me for the joy of our reunion. For three months, I saw her in memories and photos and as a blurry image on Skype. Somehow I forgot her striking beauty. With a crowd of Indians gawking, we hugged, and then made our way to a cab.

I gave the driver Jesse's address in the Abids district, then we loaded our backpacks into the trunk and climbed inside. As we sat beside each other holdings hands, I couldn't stop looking at her. An occasional headlight flashed through a window, lighting her face for a moment then just as quickly casting it back into the shadows.

"The flight went well?" I asked.

She nodded and said, "Just long."

"I imagine you're pretty tired then."

She chuckled softly. "I probably should be, but I'm not."

"Same here," I said with a smirk.

"Did you sleep at all?"

"Not really. I couldn't wait to see you."

She smiled. "Yeah, it's kinda crazy to be together—and in India of all places."

"Yeah. It is. It's even better than I imagined."

Alissa squeezed my hand. "So much better."

At Jesse's apartment, I softly knocked the front door and it cracked open. I introduced Jesse to Alissa, then he quietly led us through his family's crowded living room and into his bedroom. A red and blue tapestry hung against the back wall, and a pile of dirty clothes sat in the corner. The carpet looked like it'd never been vacuumed.

"You can stay here," he said.

"Are you sure?" I asked. "Where are you going to sleep?"

"Of course," he said, bobbling his head. "I'll sleep on the couch in the living room."

We thanked Jesse and shut the door. It was our first time alone in over three months. For some reason I felt nervous, like we were on our first date or something.

We started by sitting beside each other on the futon. But we were exhausted and ended up reclining across from one another, staring into each other's eyes. Behind Alissa, a window opened onto the navy-blue, almost ink-black sky. I shifted from the window back to her eyes. "I still can't believe we're finally together," I said with a nervous laugh. "It feels surreal."

She smiled and said, "Me neither." A strand of hair fell in front of her face, swaying with a breeze created by the overhead fan. I reached toward her and brushed it behind her ear. "Thank you."

For a while, I watched as the sky came to life, growing arctic blue with a shade of blush. Then I turned onto my back. Looking at the ceiling, I wanted so badly to kiss her. The moment didn't feel right, though. Until I told her about my past, I didn't feel comfortable sharing that level of intimacy. I wanted to make sure she could handle it—and I didn't want her regretting anything.

Eventually, I rolled off the bed and stood up. "I'll be right outside in the living room, sleeping on the floor, I guess." She didn't respond so I figured she'd fallen asleep. I tiptoed to the door, but before leaving I turned back. Against Alissa's profile, plumes of rose-colored clouds billowed upward into the sky. I couldn't imagine feeling happier. Or more nervous.

AFTER RESTING AT JESSE'S APARTMENT, ALISSA AND I HEADED OUTside where I introduced her to the bedlam of India. Wandering through narrow, busy streets, we found a restaurant serving dosa and tea. Then we took a rickshaw to the Charminar, a historic monument with four towering minarets overlooking the old city. We climbed a narrow staircase to the top and made our way around the structure as hordes of kids mobbed us.

Then we walked down the street to the Laad Bazaar, a market bustling with activity where we observed one wild sight after another. An array of vehicles wedged through the crowd, each blaring a unique horn—from squeaks to screeches to squeals to shrieks to yelps to blares to booms to bells. Beggars without limbs sat on the pavement, pleading for rupees. Vendors hawked every imaginable product. Kids swarmed us, practicing their English and shaking our hands. Then there were the women wearing full burkas who asked to take photos with us. We eagerly complied.

"What do you think?" I said at one point.

Alissa glanced at me while lifting her forehead. "Crazy crazy."

"Yup," I said with a nod. "I love it."

As afternoon faded into evening, we returned to the Hyderabad airport. The plan was to spend the next five days in Goa—widely considered India's most beautiful state. The point wasn't to sightsee or stay at fancy hotels. We simply wanted to be together.

By the time we landed in Goa, our first day together neared an end. A crowd of taxicab drivers huddled around the baggage claim, waiting to pick up passengers. After negotiating for the best price, we followed a driver to his car and got inside. Alissa leaned against me, resting her head on my shoulder, and I wrapped an arm around her. Then I began softly kissing the side of her head. Her hair smelled like strawberries.

"How are you feeling?" I asked.

"Wired," she said.

"Me too. You think you'll be able to sleep tonight?"

"Nope," she said with a laugh. "How about you?"

"Not a second."

For a while we didn't say anything. Out the window, we passed rows of palm trees. If it hadn't been dark, we probably could have seen the ocean further out. It was a moonless night, and the only light came from the Milky Way stretched across the sky.

Then I remembered what I needed to say. And I wondered if I really had to bring it up. Maybe I could put it off until the end of the trip or when we reunited back in DC. Or maybe I didn't need to tell her at all. It didn't really matter—I'd already processed the trauma and moved on.

Immediately I caught myself. Of course I needed to tell her. Not only did she have a right to know, but I needed to make sure she could accept everything about me, including my past. Only by sharing my deepest pain—and vice versa—could we experience true intimacy. Otherwise, we didn't really know each other. We hadn't let down our guard. And the love I wanted, the love I needed, didn't hide anything. In the midst of brokenness, it loved with abandon.

After a deep sigh, I said, "So, there's something I need to tell you."

"Okay," Alissa said quietly, almost nervously. "Is everything alright?"

"Yeah. Everything's perfect. I just, well, want to share something about my past. Something that's actually pretty tough to talk about."

Alissa turned and looked at me, her eyes uncertain. "Oh gosh, Paul. Are you sure?"

"Well, yeah." I paused a few seconds. "I mean, I think so. That's sorta where we're at, isn't it? Like, in our relationship."

Alissa nodded and said, "Yeah. I guess so. I was kinda hoping you'd forgotten I had something to tell you too. You know, about my past."

I chuckled. "Oh no. I'm expecting an autobiography. Every devastating detail."

"Right," she said, forcing a laugh. "From the moment of conception."

After laughing again, Alissa leaned back against me and the car grew quiet. Neither of us spoke, and I wondered if I'd missed my opportunity. Alissa finally broke the silence.

"Just don't feel any pressure," she said, rubbing my arm. "Whenever you're ready."

I took another deep breath. "Thanks."

But I didn't say anything else. For the rest of the drive, in fact, I remained silent. In my mind, though, I rehearsed what I would say.

An hour and a half after getting into the cab, we pulled up to our hotel—a small two-story building surrounding a tropical garden. I paid the driver, then we headed inside and got two rooms. Alissa wanted to clean up, so I went to my room and took a quick—and cold—shower.

Ten minutes later, I heard a knock at the door. I opened it and almost couldn't believe what I saw. Alissa with damp hair wearing short blue cotton shorts and a stretched-out white t-shirt. It felt like a dream.

"Hi," she said, a little embarrassed.

"Hi," I said with a smile. "Are you real?"

Alissa laughed. "As real as you."

She stepped into my room, and while looking out a window, I sat on the bed. For a minute I thought through what I needed to say. Then I cleared my throat.

"So…the thing I wanted to tell you," I said, pausing to take a deep breath.

Alissa turned from the window and sat beside me. She looked concerned and I thought I spotted fear in her eyes. "It's alright, Paul," she said softly. "You can trust me."

I took another deep breath as a wave of emotion squeezed my throat. I tried to speak but couldn't. Then I swallowed hard and continued, "Well, when I was fourteen, I, uh…." I stopped again and inhaled deeply.

"It's okay, Paul," she said, rubbing my back.

I smiled uncomfortably, then sighed while shaking my head. "This older guy, he…well," I paused and took a deep breath, "…abused me."

Alissa's face dropped. "Oh, Paul."

I looked away and lowered my face into my hands. "Yeah…" Then I looked at her and tried to smile but couldn't. "He was this guy I really admired, and more than anything I wanted to be his friend. I thought he was someone I could trust, someone I could look up to. But he exploited that trust and victimized me. And so badly I wish I could go back in time and keep it from happening—tell myself I didn't need to take it, he wasn't really my friend, I deserved so much better. I've thought about it a million times, but I can't change what happened." I sighed again. "I just can't."

"I know," Alissa said, nodding slowly. Her eyes teared over and she sniffled. Then she said the only words I ever wanted to hear. "I'm so sorry, Paul." She wrapped her arms around me and hugged tight. And I never felt so understood.

After pulling away, I said, "So that's kinda the big thing I wanted to tell you. There are more details if you want to know, but that's the gist. It's taken a long time to admit what happened, like until just last year. But in that time I've experienced a lot of healing, talking with friends and working with a counselor. I really do feel God's grace through it all."

Alissa nodded, and as she did, a tear slipped down her cheek.

"Don't cry," I said, smiling softly. I wiped her cheek with my hand. "I'm okay now. I really am."

"I just feel so sad for you," she said. "That you had to go through that."

I forced a smile and said, "Yeah. Me too." After a moment, "Honestly, though, I believe God has a purpose for it. Not that he planned it to happen or anything. But that somehow he's going to turn it into something good."

"I know, Paul. I believe that too. But still, it breaks my heart."

I nodded. "You're right." Then I drew a breath. "Do you have any questions?"

Alissa tilted her head and appeared to think. "No. I don't."

"Okay," I said, a little surprised. "Well, does it change, like, how you think of me?"

"Seriously?" Alissa shook her head.

I shrugged and said, "I don't know."

"Paul, of course not. It doesn't change anything."

"Really? Nothing? Like, you don't think that makes me weird or anything?"

"What? Because some twisted man abused you when you were younger?"

"Yeah. I guess. I don't know."

"No, Paul. It doesn't change how I think of you. If anything, it makes me care for you even more. And the fact that you told me, it makes me see you as even more of a man."

"Really?" I asked, almost not believing her.

"Yes. Really."

I thought about what she said for a minute, and honestly, I didn't know how to respond. Never did I expect to hear such gracious and loving words. I guess that's the lie shame had told me. That I had been so damaged no one could accept me if they learned the truth. That I could never be fully loved. But Alissa was showing me that wasn't true. I hadn't been irreparably damaged. I was accepted.

I breathed in and exhaled. And I felt such a sense of relief—a burden lifted from my conscience. "Thank you," I finally said. "You have no idea what that means to me." She smiled. Then I did what I had waited three painfully long months to do.

I kissed Alissa.

THE REMAINING FIVE DAYS PASSED IN A BLUR—A FLURRY OF ADVENTURE and romance, conversation and activity. Every day we walked along the Arabian Sea, talking while watching waves crash against abandoned beaches. Every night we ate at a local restaurant, and once we drank too much and laughed about stupid jokes. When Alissa opened up, telling me about her past, I tried to demonstrate as much grace and understanding as she showed me. Through her tears, my heart broke. But it also expanded.

Toward the end of the week, we took a series of buses from one city to another. While transferring, I stepped in a pile of cow dung the size of a pizza. The poop smeared around my flip-flop and onto my foot. Alissa's out-of-control laughter made it worth it. Later that afternoon, we got stranded at a roadside shop during a monsoon. I refused to stay in a dump with Alissa and I wouldn't let a rickshaw driver take advantage of us by charging more than the going rate. While waiting out the storm, I watched her interact with the shop owner. The love she showed that woman, asking questions and expressing genuine interest, amazed me.

We eventually found the perfect place—an old mansion converted into a guesthouse. As I stood behind Alissa listening to raindrops patter outside an open window and watching lace curtains dance with the wind's caress, I felt closer to love than ever before.

On our last night, we flew back to Hyderabad and dreamed of our future together—where we would get married, where we would live, and what our children would look like. At the airport, we enjoyed ice cream cones while basking in the glow of our growing love. We couldn't stop laughing and smiling and, when no one was looking, sneaking a kiss.

Then, after embracing for the last time in India, she left—through the airport, onto an airplane, and off to Kenya.

To my surprise, I didn't feel sad. The future appeared too bright.

LATER THAT NIGHT, I OPENED MY JOURNAL AND FOUND A POSTCARD inside. I took it out, flipped it over, and slowly read the beautifully written words.

Paul,

What an adventurous week! Thank you so much for letting me butt-in on the end of your journey. I had so much fun exploring India and, more importantly, spending time with you. Opening your heart like you did—and letting me open mine—means the world to me. Thanks for trusting me. I know I can trust you. I hope you know you're everything I've always wanted in a man. Smart, good-looking, witty, artistic, principled, faithful, and full of adventure. I feel blessed to be your girlfriend. And I can't wait to see what God's up to.

Yours truly,
Alissa

TWO DAYS LATER, I RETURNED ALONE TO THE HYDERABAD AIRPORT. With my grey, beat-up backpack and flattened charcoal fedora, I got on an airplane and flew to Bombay. From there I flew west to New York City. Then I flew to Portland. And just like I began my trip, I ended it by hugging my parents at the airport.

Much had changed in three months, though. I wasn't the same person as before. In fact, I didn't even look the same. I lost twenty pounds and added five inches to my now chin-length hair. Plus, I took over 4,000 photographs, filled a leather journal with thoughts and musings about each day's travels, read twenty books—mostly fiction and memoir—and prayed through many of the Psalms.

All of this changed me. But it wasn't the primary reason I changed. What changed me were the experiences—the daily, hourly, minute-by-minute experiences of traveling with strangers, with new and old friends, with Eko, with David, with James, with Alissa, with only myself. That's what changed me because that's where God showed up. Through each and every interaction, God spoke into my life. He prompted me to not merely confront my past, everything I wanted to avoid and ignore and bypass, but to learn and heal and grow.

And I did—I learned and healed and grew. And now, I felt prepared to step into the future as a new man.

PART FOUR
UNITED STATES

15

ATTEMPT LIFE

There's nothing quite like returning home after a long trip. During my three-month adventure, I felt like a hunter on the prowl. Food, water, shelter, and everything else fell prey to my search. And often what I hunted down wasn't what I wanted or needed.

At home, though, I didn't need to worry. Everything was clean and available. More than that, I felt comfortable. Which at first seemed strange. I'd gotten used to being on guard and analyzing every situation to determine the risks. It took a while to relax.

It also didn't help that the day after I returned, I came down with an illness that left me house-ridden for two weeks—without strength or motivation. Eventually I mustered the energy to begin writing, connecting with friends, and spending time with my family. I also had to get ready for my move to Jackson, Mississippi—a place I'd only driven through once. That meant packing my stuff again, finding a place to live, and preparing for my job as a law clerk.

I hadn't thought about the law since the bar exam. Now I needed to re-familiarize myself with it. The expectations of a law clerk are high, and I'm never one to take the easy road. It wasn't like studying for the bar, but I read a fair share of judicial opinions and law school outlines.

Then there was Alissa. Never before had I felt so strongly about a relationship. At the same time, I could tell our lives were splitting apart. To a degree it seemed inevitable. She spent her days counseling victims of sexual assault in Kenya, work that tore at the core of her being. I tried to encourage her, but I could tell the experience weighed heavy on her. It seemed to make her more serious—and less consumed with our relationship.

Our emails didn't overflow with as much emotion. Our chats over Skype didn't last as long. She had a hard time, I suspected, communicating the severity of her daily life. The tragedy and devastation she witnessed didn't lend itself to conversation.

Not that any of this surprised me. Her work demanded everything, and I was busy living my life. I knew what we had, though. Once we reunited, we would pick up where we left off in India. She assured me of the same thing. So I didn't worry.

Six weeks after stepping off a plane in Oregon, I loaded all my belongings into a trailer and began the long drive to Mississippi. As I pulled away from my parents' house, I remembered driving away so many times before—heading to college, moving to DC, leaving for my trip around the world. And this time, for some reason, it felt different.

Sadness doesn't quite capture the feeling. Loss, I think, is more apt. I don't mean in a negative sort of way. But how I imagine everyone hopes to feel at the end of a well-lived life—deeply satisfied yet tinged with grief, because everything that's come before is passing away. Gone. Over. In the distance. And there's no returning.

That's how I felt leaving Oregon. I didn't need to leave, like so many times before. I wasn't running away. I wasn't trying to hide. I left because my future took me elsewhere. It led along a different path. And somehow I sensed I would never again call Oregon home. So I grieved that passing.

At the same time, I looked forward to the journey ahead—even though I now knew I could never truly *start fresh*. There's no such thing as beginning again. Even in a new city. Every moment from my long and complicated history would follow me wherever I went. I could fight it or I could embrace it.

And I wanted to embrace my story. The good and the bad. The joyful and the tragic. Each piece. Every last bit. Because all of it made me who I had become. And that would always remain, no matter where I traveled or where I moved.

If I learned anything during my travels across the globe, it was that. Which is funny if you think about it. I needed to travel far away, attempt life on the other side of the world, to find I couldn't get away from myself. If I wanted a life of wholeness and joy, I needed to make peace with who I was—everything I'd been through.

So as I drove across the country, through Western mountains and Midwestern prairies, along wide open plains and southern forests, I wasn't fleeing anyone or anything—not Adam, not Eko, not my brothers, not my parents, not some girl, not myself, and definitely not my past.

I was simply stepping forward into my future.

IT'S EASY TO MISS JACKSON WHEN YOU'RE DRIVING ALONG INTERSTATE 20. There are few tall buildings downtown and little traffic passing through. But in its own quaint way, it's instantly beautiful. Pine trees line bronze-tinted streets and oil-lit lamps flicker outside historic homes. I moved to Jackson for one clear reason, though. For a judicial clerkship.

The way a clerkship works is like this: there are hundreds of federal and state court judges around the country. But their staffs are lean. As a result, judges rely on recent law school grads to keep their chambers running. Most are a year long, and it's highly competitive and hard to land one, particularly with judges on the higher federal courts.

All that to say, when I got an offer from a well-respected judge on the US Court of Appeals for the Fifth Circuit, I won the lottery. That it would take me to Mississippi for a year didn't matter. If anything, I liked the idea of living in the south for a while. It sounded radically different than DC—quiet, slow, relaxed. The sort of life I wanted.

So, without hesitation, I took the opportunity. The door opened for a reason. God had a purpose. I sensed it deep within.

TWO DAYS AFTER MOVING INTO MY APARTMENT IN JACKSON, I FLEW to DC to welcome Alissa back from her summer internship in Kenya. We hadn't seen each other since India two months before. It seemed longer. I now lived in Mississippi and stood at the threshold of a new life as an attorney. She had witnessed a lifetime's worth of trauma and suffering, and in days she would begin her second year of law school.

These changes didn't matter, though. Our relationship was headed toward marriage and nothing could keep us from it. My story only made sense with us together—Alissa said the same thing about her life. In light of all I'd been through over the past six years, it seemed obvious what God was doing.

That we only had three-and-a-half days together before I returned to Jackson felt unfair. What we really needed was more time. That, unfortunately, wasn't possible. So we'd have to make the best of it. With that in mind, I jam-packed our schedule with lunches and dinners and various outings. We'd be busy, but we'd have a great time.

As I pulled into Reagan National Airport, I got a text from Alissa. Her flight had been delayed and she wouldn't get in for another three hours. I pulled a quick U-turn and returned to my old roommates' house in the Atlas District.

After crashing on a couch for a couple hours, I returned to Reagan but parked in the wrong garage. Running down hallways and along people-movers, I reached the arrival area after she'd already passed through. Quickly, I raced down to the luggage claim.

That's when I saw Alissa again. She looked exhausted—and upset. I gave her a hug and handed her a bouquet of flowers.

"That's sweet," she said, feigning a smile.

"It's great to see you. I've missed you."

"Yeah, it's good to see you too."

"Is everything alright?"

She sighed. "The airline lost my luggage."

"Oh no. Is there anything we can do?"

"Yeah. Wait in this line and file a report."

I looked at the line and saw more than a dozen people in front of us. Then I looked at my phone. It was two o'clock in the morning. No wonder Alissa looked peeved.

For the next hour, we didn't say much. What can you really talk about when you've been gone for two months and all you want is to sleep in your own bed? So I didn't bother her with questions or conversation.

An hour later, I dropped her off at her friend's place and told her I'd see her in the morning. When I returned seven hours later, I found her on the verge of tears. I tried to cheer her up but she wouldn't have it. She just wanted her luggage.

"I've got an awesome day planned for us," I said.

She tilted her head. "What?"

"You'll see."

The truth is, I didn't have much on the agenda. We stopped by our favorite sights, ate lunch and dinner at our favorite restaurants, and hung out with some old friends. At one point, I told her she's the best girlfriend.

"Do you ever wonder how our relationship compares to other relationships?"

I didn't know what to say. "Well, no. I mean, I've dated enough girls to know that what we have is special. Why, how does it compare to your other relationships?"

She bit her lower lip. "It's different."

"Different? How so?"

She looked away and said, "I'm not sure. Just different."

As we said goodbye that night, I sensed I'd gotten a peak at a side of Alissa she'd kept hidden. And that worried me, because

I thought I knew everything about her. I thought her feelings for me were air-tight—perhaps stronger than my feelings for her. Now it seemed she harbored doubts. Maybe I was wrong.

"Is everything okay?" I asked before leaving.

"I don't know," she said with a sigh. "I'll feel better in the morning."

As soon as I woke the next morning, I called Alissa. Her voice told me something wasn't right. She sounded irritated—she still didn't have her luggage and I feared she resented having to spend the day with me.

I raced over to her place to fix the situation. I asked what was wrong but she wouldn't tell me. I asked how I could make her feel better but she didn't say. I tried to affirm her and encourage her and tell her how much I cared for her. But every time I spoke it made matters worse. Nothing helped. And I started to panic.

Still, we spent the day together, going through the motions—holding hands, seeing friends, engaging in shallow conversation. While eating dinner at a friends' house, she began flirting with me. It lifted my hopes and I wondered if she'd emerged from the fog.

After dinner we stopped at a bar to get drinks. I wanted to connect and remind her why she liked me, so I asked a series of introspective questions. One was whether she felt comfortable around me.

I could tell she didn't want to answer. "I don't know. Sort of."

"Really? Like on a scale of one to ten, what would you say?"

She looked away and seemed to weigh the options.

"It's okay," I said. "You can tell me. I'm tough."

"Five," she said, smiling awkwardly. "Maybe six."

"Wow. Are you serious?"

She nodded, her face uneasy.

"That's crazy. I'm at like a nine around you."

"Yeah," she said. "I can tell."

Later, she asked what I was like in college. I told her I was mostly into politics, schoolwork, Bible studies, and friends. Not a stereotypical college experience, I said, but I had fun and enjoyed it.

She almost scoffed. "Didn't you ever party?"

I pretended to think about her question but didn't need to. "No. I mean, not anything crazy."

"You would've hated me."

"That's not true. Why would you say that?"

"I partied, Paul. You didn't."

"So what? Why does that matter?"

She sighed. "I don't know. It just does. Just like it matters that you'll probably never get a tattoo."

I laughed at the ridiculousness of the statement. "You're right, I probably won't. But again, I'm not sure what difference that makes."

After paying our tab, we walked across the street to a movie theater. As we waited for the film to begin, Alissa asked how many children I wanted.

"I don't know," I said. "Maybe three. Or four. Why? How many do you want?"

"I'm not sure I want kids."

"Really?" Alissa had never mentioned not wanting kids. In fact, in India she expressed excitement about having a big family. I always pictured her as an amazing mother.

"Yeah. Really. Does that change how you feel about me?"

"Of course not. I mean, I like who you are today. Right now. Whatever happens in the future we can work through."

Once the lights dimmed, I reached for Alissa's hand—but she pulled it away. My stomach dropped. I struggled to pay attention to the movie. My world was collapsing. All my dreams were crashing around me. And I didn't know how to keep them from shattering.

After the movie, Alissa and I took the Metro to her apartment. Sitting beside each other, I reached my arm around her shoulder. Like a reflex, she leaned away.

"Not now, Paul."

"What's going on with you?" I asked, probably for the tenth time that day. "Are you feeling okay?"

"Ugh," she groaned. "All this talk of feelings is making me tired."

We didn't speak for the rest of the train ride. I didn't know what to say. I didn't want to antagonize her and make the situation worse. So I sat in silence, marinating in confusion and pain.

Alissa seemed like a different person, unrecognizable from the girl I shared my heart with in India eight weeks earlier—the girl I thought I'd fallen in love with over the past year. How could she suddenly act so insensitive and uncaring, disengaged and unaffectionate, condescending and mean?

After saying goodbye at her apartment, I walked across Capitol Hill to my old roommates' house. Not because I wanted to go for a three-mile evening walk, but because she didn't want to give me a ride. It felt like a stab to the gut after a thousand paper cuts.

WHEN I WOKE IN THE MORNING, I DIDN'T WANT TO GET OUT OF BED. I feared Alissa would pull the pin, exploding our relationship. It was my final full day in DC, though, and I still hoped to repair what apparently broke while she was in Kenya.

But it didn't seem like I could. Even after we managed to have a decent day together, our relationship felt more uncertain than ever. We ended the night sitting on the back of the Lincoln Memorial, overlooking the hills of Arlington National Cemetery.

I thought long and hard about how to create a pathway back to what we had in India. The realization it might not be possible felt like breathing water. I had never felt so emotionally unstable, so vulnerable and weak. I didn't want to act from those fears and insecurities, but I didn't know any other way.

After an extended silence, I asked if she felt better. She didn't want to talk about it, she said. I told her I deserved to know what was going on, why she was treating me so badly.

So she told me. And each word drove a nail in the lid of my coffin. She didn't know whether she wanted to be with me anymore. She didn't know if she wanted the future we dreamed about. She might not even want kids and she may want a career. She didn't want to lose control by committing to me. She didn't want to endure a year of long-distance dating. In light of her doubts, it didn't seem worth it.

I tried to reassure her by telling her we could work through all of those issues. She's what mattered—not kids, not where we lived, not our careers. I didn't care about any of that. I only cared about her.

Eventually, we left the Lincoln Memorial and walked among the Vietnam and Korean War memorials. At one point she slipped her hand into mine. I felt a hint of hope and my mind wandered.

"I know you're confused right now," I said. "I definitely am. But I hope we can work through it."

"I'm sorry, Paul," she said. "To put you through all this uncertainty. I just don't know if I can do it anymore."

"Why, though? What happened between now and a few days ago when you were telling me you couldn't wait to see me? How have things changed so dramatically since India?"

We continued walking through the shrouded memorials, by statues of lives long past. Then she said, "I don't know."

"It's strange. The way you look at me, honestly, I wonder if you even like me anymore."

She frowned and for a moment I thought my words got through to her. "I really am sorry, Paul. That makes me sad."

"How do you think I feel?" I let go of her hand and took a deep breath. "Here's the deal, Alissa. You need to make a decision based not on what you think will make me happy, but on what you want and what you believe God wants for your life. And maybe—as hard as it is for me to say—that doesn't include me."

Alissa didn't say anything back. She just nodded.

ON MY FINAL MORNING IN DC, ALISSA AND I DRANK TEA AT FOLGER
Park on Capitol Hill. Then we ate lunch at Taylor Gourmet on
H Street and returned to my old roommates' house. I picked up a
guitar and started strumming, and she sat at a piano and played
along with me. As we ran through a few hymns, I fought back
tears.

> Be Thou my Vision, O Lord of my heart;
> Naught be all else to me, save that Thou art;
> Thou my best Thought, by day or by night,
> Waking or sleeping, Thy presence my light.

Then we got into a borrowed car and began driving to the
Baltimore-Washington airport. We traveled in silence down the
highway. A barrier of oak trees lined both sides of the road. Two
lanes of light traffic extended in front of us. I struggled to keep
my eyes from overflowing with tears.

"This may be the last time we see each other," I said.

I wanted her to say something—to tell me I was crazy, that
we would see each other next weekend or the weekend after.
That we would work through whatever stood between us. That
we cared for each other too much to let our relationship shrivel
into nothing and blow away like ash.

But she didn't. Other than the sound of tires rolling over
pavement, the car remained silent. I didn't understand how she
could throw away everything we felt, everything we experienced,
everything we created, without a shred of emotion.

"What'd you enjoy most about our time together in India?" I
said after a while. It was the only question I thought to ask, perhaps because it captured the very best of our relationship—when
we thought we'd stumbled upon a lifetime of love.

Slowly shaking her head, she exhaled a sigh. "I'm not sure, Paul."

I took a deep breath. "For me, it was you." I paused, breathing in again and exhaling. "Just being with you." I looked at her and, for a brief moment, we made eye contact.

A pained smile lifted her lips. "Yeah," she said softly. "We had a good run, didn't we?"

I paused, the sadness too strong to speak. "I'll never forget it."

"Neither will I." After the words left her mouth, she bit her bottom lip and looked down.

Tightening my jaw, I forced my eyes to remain straight ahead. I wasn't just witnessing the end of our relationship, but the destruction of my dreams. We were supposed to fall in love. We were supposed to get married. We were supposed to create a life and raise a family and grow old and one day die together. But like a sandcastle breached by the ocean's tide, it disappeared forever.

When we arrived at the airport, I pulled the car next to the curb and asked if I could pray. Alissa nodded. With a shaky voice, I asked God to bless Alissa throughout the rest of her life. I asked him to care for her and protect her. I thanked him for giving me the privilege of knowing her. And I asked him to help her find what she was looking for.

Then I stepped out of the car, removed my suitcase from the trunk, and looked at Alissa standing beside me. She looked so beautiful, and in that moment I wanted nothing more than to erase the last few days and start over. But I couldn't—and maybe it wouldn't matter anyway. So for the last time, I wrapped my arms around Alissa and held tight. Then I let go and watched her get into the car and drive away.

My throat tightened and my eyes filled with tears as I made my way through security and to my gate. The flight was already boarding, so I found my place in line, handed the agent my ticket, and continued onto the plane. At my seat, I raised my suitcase into the overhead compartment and sat down.

As the airplane accelerated down the runway and lifted into the sky, I took a deep breath and exhaled.

I FELT LIKE A ZOMBIE THE NEXT COUPLE OF MONTHS—STUCK BETWEEN the land of the living and the dead. Everything felt dark. Nothing gave me joy. Even my job as a law clerk seemed pointless.

Several times I reached out to Alissa. A few times by email and twice by phone. But every time she made it clear. She didn't feel anything. She didn't want to be with me. She'd moved on with her life. Our relationship was over, and I needed to deal with it.

It was tough to accept. There were many tears shed on my knees in prayer. For so long, I believed I knew God's story for my life. I knew what he was doing and where he was leading me, as if I had peeked at the box-top and knew where each puzzle piece fit. But I didn't know anything. I never had a clue.

It's one thing to look back on life and see God's fingerprints on this event or that relationship. It's easy to trace the points of your past into a beautiful picture. Something truly divine.

Looking forward, though, it's impossible. Life only makes sense in retrospect. The picture emerges after the fact. The story takes form once it's over. In the moment, life often feels random and senseless, like an unedited reality show. No matter how close we grow to God, how near we feel to his purpose, the future will forever remain life's greatest mystery.

The best I could do was let go of my plans, those painfully naive fantasies, and step into the future. With courage and confidence and conviction that every disappointment, every failure, every heartbreak had been in preparation for something better. Something unexpected. Something beyond anything I could ever imagine.

That's the most basic and fundamental lesson of life I am learning. Every experience while traveling whispered its truth. It's the heartbeat of redemption. God taking brokenness and slowly molding something beautiful. Like watching a sunset over breaking waves, it will one day compel me to stop in awe—and worship God's majestic display of creativity and love.

At the time I had a hard time believing it. But I kept telling myself anyway.

IN THE MIDST OF ALL THIS, I WENT TO LUNCH ONE AFTERNOON WITH some of the other judge's law clerks. I'd met a few of them already, but not everyone. The job was demanding and didn't leave much time to socialize. Part of me didn't want to be around anyone—I preferred eating alone where I could sulk in my sorrows. But I went, knowing I had to eventually reenter the world.

A group of us met outside the courthouse on Capitol Street and began walking west toward the Mayflower Café. It was hot and not a cloud dotted the endless blue sky. As we walked along the sidewalk under the sun's pounding heat, my friend Cody introduced me to one of his co-clerks.

"Hi, I'm Hilary," she said with a radiant smile. She had shoulder-length blonde hair, striking bright blue eyes, and a beautiful face. If I hadn't been steeped in heartbreak I would've been interested. But I didn't even think about it. I couldn't.

We shook hands and I said, "I'm Paul. Great to meet you."

And then we continued heading down the street toward the Mayflower.

It's interesting, because at the time I didn't think much about meeting Hilary. It certainly never crossed my mind that in six months we would begin dating, and later that year I would tell her I loved her, and a year after that I would propose to her, and five months later we would get married, and two-and-a-half years after that we would welcome our daughter into the world.

But that's precisely what happened. Now, looking back, it all seems so obvious. This was always God's story. And every day I'm thankful he's the author and I'm not.

ACKNOWLEDGMENTS

First and foremost, I'm grateful for my wife, Hilary Perkins. Without you, this book would not exist. I wrote the first few chapters while we dated; the first draft during the first six months of our marriage; an entire rewrite after you became pregnant; and I edited the manuscript during your third trimester. Through it all, you were not only endlessly patient and encouraging, but *helpful* (i.e., you're a great editor). Thank you, Hilary. You're the love of my life and my best friend.

I also want to thank our daughter, Clara. Even though you entered the world after this book was written, I penned it with you in mind—because one day you will read it. And I want you to be proud.

I could not be more thankful for my parents, Bill and Cindy Perkins—for your love and support and encouragement and... well, everything. I owe you my life, and I'm so blessed to have you as my mom and dad. Thank you, Dad, for your countless hours of editing. This book is significantly better because of your contributions.

My two brothers, Ryan and David, encouraged me through the process, and David in particular helped by editing "Memories with My Brother"—it wasn't always easy, but I hope you're pleased with the finished product. Thank you both for your love and support.

My gratitude goes to my counselor, Jim Badorrek. Although he only makes a passing reference in this book, his wisdom and insights influenced every chapter, particularly the second-to-last paragraph. Thank you for helping me understand God's story for my life. I also want to thank Tommy Hinson, who supported when I first began working through these issues.

There are several people who read drafts or excerpts and deserve my appreciation. Joshua Rogers—I'm thankful for your feedback. Ryan Cole—your encouragement lifted me when I doubted. Tim Goeglein—your advice and support was invaluable. And Debbie Akhbari—who planted the seed of this book by asking a single question: "How did you enjoy Bali?"

An enormous amount of credit goes to my esteemed agent, David Van Diest. Thank you for believing in this story—and for continuing to believe even after I'd given up.

I will forever count my editor, Judith Dinsmore, as a hero. You helped mold a string of stories into a single story. Thank you for your hard work—and for putting your heart into my story. I am deeply indebted to you.

I am thankful for the entire team at Whitaker House—Bob Whitaker, Christine Whitaker, Tom Cox, Cathy Hickling, and Becky Speer. Thanks for taking a chance with me. I especially want to thank Don Milam, whose early support was a game changer.

Finally, I want to thank you—for letting me into your life. It's truly an honor and privilege. I can only hope my words have meant as much to you as they mean to me.

ABOUT THE AUTHOR

Paul Perkins grew up outside of Portland, Oregon. After graduating from Oregon State University, he moved to Washington, DC, and worked in the US Senate and then at the White House. Later, he graduated from The George Washington University Law School and clerked on the US Court of Appeals for the Fifth Circuit.

Paul is now an attorney in Washington, DC, where he lives with his wife and daughter. His writing has been featured at *The Huffington Post, Boundless,* and *RELEVANT.* In 2016, one of his articles was nominated for the Evangelical Press Association's Higher Goal award.

paulperkins.com
#unexpectedjourneysbook

UNEXPECTEDJOURNEYSBOOK.COM